RECOVERY IS POSSIBLE

AN ADDICT'S STORY

BY

MATT PENN

Contents

Dear younger self,

I am sorry you went through what you did through no fault of your own, and as a result, some of the choices you made hurt yourself and others.

I'm sorry you never felt worthy and did not believe in yourself.

And I'm sorry you felt locked away in a prison of shadows, cold and alone.

But I want you to know that you did the best you could to cope, using the limited knowledge you had.

And you will get through it. The sun will shine on you, little buddy.

Please do not worry, because I am at a point where I can retake control.

You are stronger than you know! And everything's going to be okay from now on.

I love you,

Your future self

Introduction

Yes! Another Day alcohol-free for me today, and I feel good. But it hasn't always been this way. After a lifetime of struggling with alcoholism, drug addiction, and solvent abuse, I decided to embark on a journey that would be my road to recovery.

I had tried many times to get myself clean and sober and failed miserably with every attempt. I had never quite been able to break away from the chains that kept me turning to a drug of some kind to cope, heal, have fun, build my confidence, ease anxieties, or simply to sleep. The list of reasons why is endless.

But I did manage to live an ordinary everyday life. In fact, many people would have thought I seemed like a proud, supportive father, a loving partner, and a good friend. However, behind closed doors, as the sun began to go down, I would change and become someone else. I am a high-functioning alcoholic.

The alcohol would change my persona. I would become selfish, aggressive, foul-mouthed, and inconsiderate – a real Jekyll and Hyde – and I would steadily intoxicate myself until I was ready to pass out. The following day, I would wake up filled with remorse and go to work, later going through the same motions again once I got home.

I have ruined relationships, lost friends, and broken hearts. But all I could ever think of was my own needs, which were a matter of survival to me. Let me just say something now. I am not a bad person by default; I know right from wrong, I work hard, I love my family, and when I describe myself as I have above, it sickens me, but it is the truth.

I am an alcoholic addict, but I am also a survivor of abandonment, child sexual abuse, and attempted murder. Later in life, I lost a child to anencephaly. These are not excuses for my behaviour; they are experiences within my past. I view these as my gateway into addiction.

On 24 May 2020, after a series of events, I decided enough was enough, and I had to bring about change. I went into recovery. As I did so, I decided to make an online video blog to track my progress. I thought that seeing my recovery might encourage others to make changes within their own lives.

A Facebook page was born called Alcohol No More, and later, I changed the name to Matt Penn, after it was pointed out to me that the phrase 'alcohol no more' could be a trigger for some people. You can follow my page at www.facebook.com/TheMattPenn

You will find videos and posts dating back to my first day alcohol-free, and this book was published to celebrate one year of sobriety.

I decided to write this book to share my story and what I did during my first year alcohol-free, hoping that it inspires you to make the changes needed within your life, whether to do with addiction or otherwise. Many of the things I discuss can be utilised in different areas or to combat other issues.

I am no counsellor, nor am I a therapist in any way. I am not a world-famous author or a celebrity of any kind. My name is Matthew Penn, and I am just an ordinary guy who wanted to share his story. I wanted to prove to myself that not only could I go through my own recovery, but I could accomplish something, and this book is a testament to that. I have tried to write from my own perspective; I do not know the science behind recovery and addiction, nor do I pretend to know. Plenty of books are already available on the subject that can fill you with facts about alcoholism and the dangers it poses to your health.

This book comes from my heart and is a labour of love. I hope I have successfully shown you the tools that helped me on my journey, such as beginning to talk and open up about my past and how I deal with triggers and cravings.

I can only share my view from my own perspective of recovery, and everyone's recovery is different. I hope, however, that this text may ignite something within you that will encourage you to seek out your own means to overcome whatever challenges you may face while also demonstrating that we are more than our past. We are more than our addictions. We can accomplish anything we set our minds to if we never give up and are prepared to go all the way.

That is what my Facebook page and this book are really about. You cannot fail as long as you keep trying and never give up. I learnt over time during Year One to view my mistakes and my failings as opportunities to learn, to succeed. This came after I read a meme saying that all successes are built on a foundation of mistakes and failures. I believe this to be true; everybody who knows success within their field will have experienced failure. They become successful because they do not give up; they stick to their goal, to their dream, and learn from those mistakes, and I believe recovery is the same.

Upon completion of this book, I realised one thing. My story, the Facebook page, and this book are not just about recovery from addiction. They are something more; they are examples that we can overcome. Sure, it's hard sometimes. We can be taken to a point where we cannot see ourselves pulling through. If we stick with our intention and goals, think outside the box, seek support, and do what needs to be done …

We can overcome anything.

Thank you so much for being here!

I love ya,

Matt x

A Note to the Reader

Before we begin, my friend, I do need to point out that if you're considering making changes within your life to clamber out of the whirlpool of addiction to alcohol or other substances, I cannot emphasise enough the importance of seeking help from a medical professional.

Everyone's recovery is different. In many cases, there is a need for a medical detox whereby the user receives their first abstinence from the substance under medical observation. This is because detoxing can be dangerous, depending on many factors, such as your consumption and current state of health.

There are several helpful organisations such as Alcoholics Anonymous, Narcotics Anonymous, and Alanon, to name just a few. A quick Google search will offer you a list of local organisations that can assist and support you. You do not need to go into recovery alone.

If you are a family member, there are also charities and organisations that can offer support and information, such as Adfam, Alanon, and Turning Point. Again, a quick Google search will show you many free resources.

If you need to talk to someone in the UK, the Samaritans can be contacted 24 hours a day on 116 123, or you can email them at jo@samaritans and contact them by snail mail at:

Chris

Freepost RSRB-KKBY-CYJK

PO Box 9090

STIRLING

FK8 2SA

A problem shared is a problem halved; there is no shame in asking for help. There is assistance out there. You will find your own recovery journey a more comfortable experience if you reach out and accept it. I know that can be difficult, but you are doing the best thing for your life, and that first contact could instigate the help that will change your life for the better.

1. Gateway

Many people think that the gateway to more problematic addictions stems from experimenting with drugs like cannabis or solvents alone. My gateway to addiction was none of these. My gateway to addiction was the childhood trauma I survived.

My addictions were my comfort. I used them to self-medicate from the memories and subconscious effects of the abandonment, sexual abuse, and attempted murder I survived as a child.

Later in life, I locked my means to self-medicate firmly into place when I lost my son Joseph to anencephaly.

I am an alcoholic addict in recovery, but it was not dabbling with drugs that opened the doorway to a life of struggling with addiction. It was my need to try to forget. It was the fear that overcame me when the night fell. I believed I needed alcohol to help get me through and cope with the struggles of life. I was wrong, and I know that now.

Please listen to me, my dear friend, when I tell you that childhood trauma is the real gateway to addiction for many. Addicts are some of the most vulnerable people in our society, yet we attack them without knowing their story.

This has to change; I urge you to listen, believe, understand, and support with kindness and empathy, and please never judge. You could save a life. This is my story ...

2. Abandonment

The definition of abandonment according to the *Collins English Dictionary*:

The abandonment of a place, thing, or person is the act of leaving it permanently or for a long time, especially when you should not do so.

On the 9th of March 1978, David Penn was born; two years later, on the 3rd of May, I came along. Two bundles of joy delivered to our parents Chris and Linda Penn. A perfect little family that would make anybody happy. Clan Penn's newest members, my brother and I, had the world at our feet. A future filled with promise and hope, just as it should be for all young children when they arrive into the arms of their loving parents. Unfortunately, however, this would not be the case. The journey that lay before us was an early life of struggle, upset, and pain in many ways. This was just a way of life for us, as I am sure it was for many growing up in Medway in those days. Gillingham, Chatham, and Rochester make up the towns that reside beside the River Medway in Kent.

I was raised in lower Gillingham, which was literally on the wrong side of the tracks. The top end of Gillingham wasn't too bad, to be fair, but if I was to describe my local area as a colour, I would say very grey; it was a very grey place to live. How else can I describe it? Let's just say that if Kent was the garden of England, Medway was the compost heap at the bottom. It was known as 'brown town' to the criminals and dealers who commuted in from London to sell their merchandise. This was because of all the heroin rife in the area – well, only rife due to those fuckers importing it to our streets. I guess that's business, supply and demand, and there was demand.

Anyway, before I had the opportunity to build any memories of my mother, she left us. Maybe she got tired of brown town, I don't know. I don't know much, to be honest, especially the exact ins and outs of her departure or the reasons why she buggered off. I don't really care anymore, either. I have heard two stories from two sides, and I will never know the truth. What I can tell you, my friend, is this. I was born two years after my brother and experienced having our mum with us for maybe a year or two before she was gone. Not dead, just gone. She left us to be with another man and start a new life.

Bully for her! Whoop de whoop. I guess we would all like the opportunity to start over, and who would want two kids in tow? I mean, that would ruin all the fun of a new relationship, wouldn't it? Maybe I'm being harsh, because, according to some, she did have a reason, and from what I can understand, that reason is that my dad was very abusive. As the old saying goes, though, there are always two sides to every story, and the other side of this tale of abandonment is the one I grew up with.

The story I know is that my mother was never happy or content with what she had, so she fucked off and left us when something better came along. I would just like to say that this isn't me having a pop at my mum or a cheap shot at her expense. I am just relaying to you how it was to build a picture in your mind's eye of our situation growing up. I really don't know what happened; let's just say, for argument's sake, it was 50/50.

Subsequently, my brother and I became wards of court. The outcome was that we went to live with my nan, granddad, and uncles in Medway. This was the family I grew up with and the only one I knew.

Growing up, my nan was my mum, and she did a great job in many respects, as I know things weren't easy for her at all. When I was a toddler, I lovingly called her Mummy Nanny, and my granddad was Grumpy Gramps. Although this was all that I knew growing up, I couldn't help but wonder where my mum was, and as I got older and more aware, I started to wonder why she had left her children.

As I became more worldly wise, I asked myself why she would leave me with a man she thought was violent or abusive. Where were her maternal instincts? If you felt abused by your ex-husband, why would you leave your children with his family where he could be a threat to them or their safety?

Being a sensitive, quiet lad growing up in David's shadow, I became a deep thinker, but thinking about my mum was difficult for me, as my nan would never speak of her. I was also afraid to ask her about my mum because I didn't want to cause any upset. I couldn't do it. I felt that by asking my nan about my mum, somehow I wasn't being loyal to her and the care she had given me since I was a baby. She had always been the one constant in my life, and I never wanted to hurt her, so I kept my questions to myself. I know my nan did her very best for us with very little, I really do, but growing up, I did often look at the door and wonder if I would get a surprise visit. Every birthday, I thought *maybe this year I'll get a card*, but nothing ever came through the letterbox.

The years rolled on, and I received nothing from anyone on my mother's side. I had other nans, granddads, aunties, possibly uncles and cousins. We had never moved house; everyone would have known where we were, yet no contact whatsoever. Who knows? Not me, that's for sure. We never heard from any of them again. As I got older, my mind became a confused, chaotic mess. Internally I began to blame myself, with self-talk like 'I must have been the reason she left! Everything was fine until I came along!' I was too young to understand, and thoughts like this can become overwhelming. As a result, in many ways, I became withdrawn.

I don't quite understand why, but I constantly apologised, saying sorry every two minutes for things that didn't warrant an apology. Sorry, sorry, sorry, SORRY!

Many people thought I was a sweet little boy. 'Matthew's no trouble,' I heard a lot. I lacked confidence, I wouldn't eat at children's parties, I was very submissive, and I allowed other kids to walk all over me. I hung back when there was a queue for the slide or if I attended parties. When all the kids were dancing, I refused to go have fun. I did want to enjoy myself – I really wanted to join in, but I just couldn't put myself out there like the other kids. Now I am older, I look back and think I was lost in many ways. The quiet, subdued little boy was going to struggle. This became evident when I encountered my first obstacles, which were primarily fitting in with the Penn way of doing things. This was a way of life that, for me, was often difficult.

My family would take pride in saying they were old school. Raised by my nan and granddad, we did have a moral code to follow that would fit nicely in an East End gangster movie. You have to be hard, tough; don't back down from anyone; punch first, ask questions later! Look after your own, respect your elders, respect women, and always stand together against anyone, including the law. My brother found it relatively easy to fit into this role and way of life. On the other hand, I struggled, and I didn't feel I had much of an identity – or at least not the identity expected of me.

Beaten up at school? Go back and face them again! There was more than one? Take them out one by one! Always hit the biggest one first, look them in the eye no matter how scared you are, and if you get knocked down, you keep getting back up! And you don't cry! Don't be a fairy! You're a Penn, for fuck sake! Not a fanny! And that's just how it was for us.

I remember one time I got beaten up over the Green (Gillingham Green, a local graveyard that also served as a park that was next door to where we lived) by a group of bigger boys. I went home crying; my granddad had a go at me and told me to go back over there and face them. Oh, what a choice – go face the bigger boys who just beat the crap out of me or face my granddad? Naturally, I went to meet them, which was far more appealing than dealing with the wrath of

Grumpy Gramps. Even his 'you're in the shit now' hundred-yard stare was enough to make me step up. Yes, indeed, I found my conkers, wiped my tears, and rather nervously wobbled my way back over there.

I didn't know it at the time, but my granddad had sent my brother behind me to protect me. He wanted to see if I would have the courage to stick up for myself. Yeah, I kind of get that now. Could I do that to Tyler, my son? No, but his world is very different from the one I grew up in, thank God. My brother David was very well known in the area for being one of the toughest kids in school. As soon as they caught sight of my brother behind me, they legged it. Yeah, motherfuckers, you better run; in that instant, I wasn't wobbling; I was striding like Bertie Big Bollocks.

Living in this family environment, I did pick up skills for our local parks and school playground's battlefields easily along the way. There was plenty for us to learn from, so it stood to reason, but I didn't want to be a fighter. There were always battles and skirmishes going on around us. Watching my dad and uncles fighting in the pub was a regular occurrence – either smashing each other up or dishing out a few slaps to some other poor sod who had knocked their pint over. One minute they'd be laughing and joking, the next minute, *boom*, the main event: the Penn boys are on one!

Often, I would be there in the trenches, ducking and witnessing these young men knocking seven shades of shit out of each other. Honestly, it was crazy shit. But even crazier still was the pattern that always followed. When things erupted and shit went down, who you gonna call? Old Bill?

No, fuck that; the landlord would call my nan and say 'Your boys are fighting again.' Like I say, crazy shit.

She was not a big woman either; she was actually tiny, but man, oh man, she was a battleaxe. I suppose she had to be, as Gramps was a captain in the merchant navy and a freeman of the River Thames. He was away at sea for most of my early life, so she had to raise and control all these boys independently. She had to be a tough cookie, bless her. My nan was the family's matriarch watching over my three uncles, my dad, my brother, and me.

One memory I have of them all together was standing on the corner of the close we lived in watching four grown men beating the shit out of each other and my nan in the middle, breaking it up. She was the only person who could stop them, and for her efforts she earned the nickname Mrs Kray after the mother of the notorious Kray twins. My nan's boys were her world, and although she wasn't afraid to clip them around the ear and drag them home when they did wrong, no matter how old or big they were, she loved us all dearly. She would happily put her life on the line for any of her kids. My nan was a prime example of unconditional love in many ways with the shit she put up with.

We were well known in Medway as a family that stuck together and who could handle themselves. As David got older, he took up his role very well as the next in line. I had a lot to live up to, but I never really wanted to be like them, and I always wondered if I took after my mum's side of the family. It wounds me to say that I felt adopted, and within myself I felt little connection; yes, I loved them all, but in my head, I just wasn't like them. There was always a drama going on. Life for us was a merry-go-round of police coming to the house and bailiffs at the door. Memories of one uncle covered in blood, another passed out on the sofa, pissed, my dad fighting the other, or my granddad paying off drug dealers. Attending prison visits and time at the hospital were all normal for my brother and me; it was an education in many ways. Training for later in life, I suppose.

Don't get me wrong, though; it wasn't all bad. As I say, those things were normal to us. If you don't know any different, it's not that bad, right? One fond memory is that there were always people at the house, especially on a Sunday. My nan would be singing in the kitchen, cooking a roast dinner. Back then, you used to smell roasts being cooked from everyone's kitchen as you walked down the street, as most people had the same routine. Our front door would be open and people would just walk in. 'Hello, Mrs Penn,' we would hear as the door opened. You never knew who would come back from the pub, and she always had a table full of people. Deliberately cooking more dinner than she needed, I think she loved having a houseful. An amazing, strong lady, she was the matriarch, no doubt.

As a child, I guess I did kinda like that, the constant comings and goings of different folks. Big blokes who you knew were quite handy coming in and making a fuss of us, slipping us a couple of quid for pocket money or coming in with toys that had fallen off the back of a lorry. Our movie collection was fantastic, filled with pirate VHS tapes of the latest Star Wars or Disney movie that someone had brought home for us. That was the way things were, growing up.

After dinner, the house would empty of men as they swaggered over to the pub. Sometimes they would take David and me with them. Back then, the pubs were always busy due to the opening times being shorter. Everyone seemed to be there after Sunday dinner, and we knew them all. The Five Bells was our local at the end of our road – Holly Close in Gillingham. We had some excellent times there, I must say, but other times we would get caught up in the middle of a pub fight – and when I say fight, I don't mean a couple of slaps. I mean bottles in faces and pool cues round heads kinda fights. Nasty, aggressive battles, the kind you would see in an old Western bar brawls, and they seemed to thrive on it.

My uncles were like brothers to us, which in many ways was great. But I think now, looking back, the problem was that was they were twenty years older than us. We were witnessing stuff we shouldn't have been involved in for at least ten or fifteen more years – if any child should be witnessing things like that at all! I know I would never want my kids to. I love all my uncles dearly, and in their own way, they were very good to David and me. But they were also young men and were going to get up to antics. Little did anyone know that the crazy goings-on of my early childhood laid the foundations for my later life. I used to hide one uncle's empty bottles of vodka for him (learning my craft young), while another uncle would take us on little excursions breaking into MOD property for an adventure. Yeah, can you believe it? As I say, crazy shit. Other kids had days out at

Thorpe Park while we were trespassing on government property and hiding from armed guards. Yay, an adventure! I I felt like one of the Goonies.

Such fun, but let me take a moment to talk about my dad. He was a different kettle of fish. My father was not a very nice man. It pains me so much to say it, but it's the truth. My uncles were fun – crazy but fun. Responsible, no ... but fun, yes. Regarding my dad, I cannot say he ever showed a fun side. No matter how hard I think, spending time with him was never fun. My brother may say different, but I do not have any happy memories of spending time with my dad when I was a child. He was never silly and only laughed at other people's expense, including mine and my brother's, which made him a bully. The way he was with people did make things difficult for me at times. I knew my dad's reputation, and it wasn't a nice one.

   He was actually a former police officer and judo champion. Yes, as a young man, he was a copper. He would not admit this later in life; he viewed himself as gangster number one. My dad used his strength and weight to make others feel threatened, to intimidate people. The problem was that he wasn't all talk and would back up his threats with his fists quite easily. I found this embarrassing, shameful, scary, and very distant from the image of the father I really wanted. I can't speak for my brother, but I think that when he was younger, he wanted to be like my dad and have his reputation. My brother was never a bully growing up, but he was a hard fucker as well. Time went on, and as brothers, we were close, but we began to move down different paths as he entered senior school, and at that time, I was going through my own hell on earth that no one was aware of.

3. Predator

The definition of predator according to the *Collins English Dictionary*:

A predator is an animal that kills and eats other animals. People sometimes refer to predatory people or organisations as predators.

Growing up, all I wanted to do was fly. I would sit and watch the birds and dream of having wings, soaring up into the clouds and beyond. My favourite bird was the kingfisher. One of my fondest memories from childhood was visiting the Norfolk Broads on holiday; it was so cool. Seeing a kingfisher darting past my eyeline with a flash of colour at random moments. So beautiful, fast and free. Yeah, I loved birds, but my real obsession growing up was planes.

All I wanted to do when I became an adult was to be a pilot in the Royal Air Force. This was a passion that I dreamed about daily, those magnificent men in their flying machines. My hero back then was Sir Douglas Bader. What a man – living proof of someone who overcame his disabilities to fly to victory against all the odds. He was taken to the brink of death after crash landing his plane, only to rejoin the RAF minus his legs, proving that we really can overcome anything and reach for the skies.

My favourite plane was the Stealth F117A fighter/bomber … which is American, but that didn't faze me. I had a plan to join the British Royal Air Force and transfer to the American Air Force. I don't quite know how that would work, an international air force transfer, but in my young mind, I would make it possible; this was my dream.

As I said previously, I was a very quiet child; I was always in my bigger brother's shadow, quite often playing alone. Sometimes I would sit in my front garden with my toy soldiers all around me. I would spend hours meticulously setting them up and arranging them for battle in all kinds of different scenarios. It sounds boring, but to me, that was the fun bit. Planning, preparing, strategising.

I lived in a tranquil little close where we knew all the neighbours, and back then, kids were out playing without the worries of today's world. The days were long, and the holidays seemed to last forever. My nan would let me go off and play over the green, just at the top where she could see me, and if need be, she would tell me what time I needed to be home for dinner and off I would trot. If I wasn't there, you would find me in the front garden in my own little world doing my own thing. My nan's garden was fantastic. She loved flowers and shrubs, and these were perfect for my many combat scenarios. She used to say that a weed is just a flower in the wrong place, something I related to, growing up.

I remember one particular day I was out front playing and this guy strolled up to me from his car, an old Capri, and started talking to me. A smart chap, mid-forties with a gentle face. Dressed like an office worker – shirt, tie, trousers. I had seen him a few times. I remember his mum lived in the bungalows at the end of our close. He wasn't really a stranger according to how we are raised to perceive people we don't know. I was still a shy little lad, though, and had difficulty talking to people I wasn't closely associated with and making new friends. But he had said hello to me a few times and always seemed to be smiling and a very gentle character.

On this day, he came over; my battlefield of plastic soldiers seemed to have attracted him. He asked me all about them and if I wanted to be a soldier when I grew up. I said, 'No, I want to be a pilot.' I was probably about eight at the time. This was the first time he'd spoken to me properly on my own. The conversation wasn't overly long, and it was just a general chit chat about what I was playing. Nothing that you would think was too out of the norm.

After that day, I began to see him more regularly in the close. I'd be playing wall ball or kurby with a friend or on my own, and he would join in, always very kind and seemingly lovely. We all thought he was a lonely man who liked to visit and look after his mum. My nan would come to the door, say hello, etc., and over time, I guess friendships were formed. I think I was ten, maybe eleven years old; I'm not entirely sure, to be honest, but some time had passed when he came to the house saying he had tickets for the Biggin Hill Air Show. He asked my nan if it would be okay if I went with him.

He was a neighbour – well, sort of; his mum was a neighbour and this was her son. A respectable chap who we knew worked for the police, and paedophiles weren't really a big thing then. Dirty old men, yes, but I never heard the word paedophile. So I guess my nan thought *okay*. She had no reason to think otherwise. Everything was okay; he didn't do anything wrong or dodgy. He spent money on me, I got to sit in planes, and it was amazing. One of the best days of my life! I sat on the roof of his car and was just in awe of those superheroes scudding about in the skies above me.

That day marked the beginning of many trips out, gradually becoming further afield to other air shows and Air Force museums. These trips evolved into days out in London with visits to the Imperial War Museum, Madame Tussauds, and West End musicals. I loved London, in fact; we went there regularly. I was caught up in the lights and the hustle and bustle; it was all so new to me and exhilarating. As time went on, we would talk. I guess he picked up on the fact that my brother was good at sport, good-looking, and strong; he was the kind of guy all the girls loved, who got a lot of attention through his football, swimming, or whatever sport he turned his hand to.

On the other hand, I was scruffy, wasn't fussed by labels, was crap at all sports, and girls most certainly only looked at me because I was David Penn's little brother (this is true; I heard one say it once). Gradually, a bond was forming, and he started calling me 'son' whenever we were away from Gillingham and the ears of my family members. I didn't mind, as he had told me he'd always wanted a little boy but never had one, and that's why he enjoyed spending time with me. I suppose I longed for a father who had time for me and was actually interested in being a normal dad.

Let me point out here that my granddad was an amazing man and a brilliant father figure; however, he was also away at sea a lot. When I was young, we didn't see much of him. My actual father, well, he just never bothered to be a father, not really, not in the way my brother and I craved. My uncles filled that role, but they were young men wanting to do their own thing in life, and they enjoyed being the fun uncles.

Over time, things began to develop, and I say develop because he didn't just suddenly rape me. The abuse started and grew without me even realising what was going on. Thinking back, it all started with a little touch on my knee, putting his arm around me, comforting me and being reassuring. I thought this was him playing the caring father figure; however, he was far from that.

The arm around me would often lower and go around my waist and towards my bottom. I just never realised what he was doing. I was very young and innocent; why would I? What I thought was a comfort, he was probably getting off on.

Eventually, the inevitable happened, and he planned a night away camping. He had all the gear, and I had never been away from my grandparents alone before. David went on holiday to Florida with his friends. Still, I had never had an opportunity like that, so I was excited to go. My nan thought all was safe, as this guy had always looked after me previously. Little did we know that this was the trip he was building up to and the opportunity for which he had been putting in all the groundwork over such a long time. He must have been drooling at the prospect of getting me away, alone and vulnerable, for one whole night. Because that is when it started, and many of my dreams were destroyed.

Everything was fine during the day; we cooked, played ball, put up the tent, and I suppose to other people we looked like father and son. It wouldn't surprise me if onlookers thought *wow, look at that amazing dad. He must have his son for the weekend.*

Night-time blanketed the world, and we were sitting in the tent when he pulled out a bottle of vodka. He said it was to warm him up and it was nice with Coke. But, oddly, it wasn't cold. He asked me if I wanted to try and, of course, said 'Don't worry, I won't tell your nan.' I had sneaked some of my uncle's beer at the pub before, to everyone's amusement. At Christmas, we were allowed a light ale with lemonade. Still, vodka … all I knew of that was the empties I used to hide for my uncle. Well, he drank a lot of it, and at the end of the day, he had been one of my role models growing up. I wanted to feel grown-up, and I trusted this man, so why not?

I was very nervous and sipped at my plastic cup very attentively. He knew this as he watched me like a hawk focused on a little field mouse scurrying home, completely unaware of the killing machine locked on and waiting for the right moment to pluck its prey from the comfort of the world, then toy with it before destroying the flesh and leaving the spirit within the darkness of the abyss.

'Come on, let's play a game I know called minute massacres. We drink as many shots as possible in a minute.' As he said this, I remember him getting undressed and getting half in his sleeping bag, saying he always had to sleep naked. I felt uncomfortable, but the alcohol was beginning to make me feel warm and giddy. This man frequently found excuses to lean over and touch me, and another weird thing that I never noticed at the time but which seems strange now is that as he spoke to me, stared at me, he would squeeze his nipple. The images of this now fill me with dread, this vile, disgusting monster.

That was the first time I drank with him, and I blacked out; I don't recall much more until the following morning. When I woke up, a pungent smell filled the tent. I could taste it, it was so strong. It was a mix of body odour, sweat, and something else, like oil or creams. I was sore around my genitals and bottom. There were broken elastic bands in the sleeping bag; looking back, I think he put them around my testicles. I went to the toilet and my bum hurt, but my hangover was taking over. I felt sick, and the headache was unbearable. My body ached all over.

He told me I must have fallen when I was drunk as he gave me some water and painkillers. 'Don't worry, I won't say anything to your nan.' Obviously, I didn't want that! And I didn't really know what had happened. Everything was a haze. I just didn't want to get in trouble, and aside from whatever had happened when I was unconscious, I had had a good time.

We went into town in the morning, and he bought me some gifts to take back. I really wanted a game all my friends had but I couldn't afford, so he made a beeline for a video game store and bought it for me, and anything else I wanted. Spoiling me to keep me quiet, and it worked. I didn't want to get in trouble, wasn't sure what had happened, but I had never had money spent on me like this before. He bought my silence, which made me feel so ashamed and dirty. As an adult, I hated myself for this and always felt as though I had sold myself to this man. These weekends became more frequent and we went to different places, although camping became caravans and caravans became hotels.

The first time I was consciously aware of what he was doing, I felt his hand come under the duvet. Bizarrely, I could hear him crying, sobbing. Still, his hand continued to subtly move its way under the sheets like a spider or a snake slithering towards its lunch. I didn't know what was going on and just allowed it to happen. The crying while he performed sex acts became a regular thing that I don't think I will ever fully understand.

His disgusting breath and tongue make me feel physically sick when I think of them today. *Vile! Yuk!*

I don't know why I didn't say anything. My dad would've killed him. He was very kind to me in the day. I had never had that before. I guess I didn't want that to end – trips out, buying me anything I wanted, and by this time I was becoming used to alcohol, so at night I was getting pissed!

But that wasn't enough for him as I got older; he began to introduce me to sniffing solvents and drugs. Well, they say sniff, but I used to inhale lighter gas directly into my mouth to the lungs. As we drove down the motorway, I'd be completely trashed while he would rub my inner thighs.

I remember one time I was under the influence, captivated by a hallucination of a giant ping-pong ball bouncing on either side of the motorway above me. When I came back to reality, we were in a secluded lay-by, my pants were down, and he was … on me. I would just go back to noo-noo land until he had finished. He would sometimes bring cannabis, but it was mainly alcohol and lighter gas at first, occasionally poppers.

This went on for years. The abuse got more imaginative as he got braver, and sometimes he came equipped with silks to tie (they leave no marks), clamps, dildos, etc. – you get the gist.

He also took me to another monster's house a few times. All I knew of him was his nickname, Gary Baldy, and he lived in Brighton. There were photos of young boys on the walls in his flat – no family pics, just all different boys. He told me he had a lot of nephews. The vodka would come out, and I don't need to go into detail here. I'm sure you know where that led. I often wonder and hope that those boys are okay. I remember their photos clearly in my mind's eye.

I've never spoken about this in such detail before, but I'm not ashamed anymore and know I did nothing wrong. The cunning and lengthy process he used to get what he wanted demonstrates the dangers our young people face and how convincing these individuals can be.

In today's world, we would say I was groomed. I feel like I was, and I was also hunted by a predator.

4. Savage

The definition of savage according to the *Collins English Dictionary*:

Someone or something that is savage is extremely cruel, violent, and uncontrolled.

I remember it like it was yesterday – well, some of it. I was thirteen years old and out with my friend and two girls. We were enjoying a typical day hanging around Chatham high street, as we all did back then. The Pentagon Centre and an indoor market that was known as Inshops were like a magnet to teenagers, and I was just starting to explore and get used to a bit of freedom.

I enjoyed days out with my friends; it allowed me an opportunity to forget about the Predator, even if it was only for a day. None of my friends was ever aware, just as my family wasn't; how could I ever tell them? It isn't the kind of thing you drop into conversation while playing Mortal Kombat on the PS or kicking a ball around.

The two girls we were with lived in Princess Park, and as it was getting late in the afternoon, being the gentleman that we were, we decided to walk the girls home. It was a bit of a journey, but we used to walk for miles in those days. It had been a good day; we hadn't upset anyone or done anything different from what normal teenage lads do. Certainly nothing that would attract any unwanted attention. Our walk would take us through Chatham high street and past what used to be Chatham cinema. This would be the location that marked an event that changed my life in the blink of an eye … forever.

One second, I would be there, and the next, I would be gone.

I would like to say I got into a fight over the girls' honour and took two grown men on in fisticuffs. Unfortunately, after a courageous battle, I nearly lost my life. The truth isn't as exciting, but I feel far more SAVAGE! All I can tell you is how things happened and what I can remember from my perspective. As I walked past the cinema holding hands with my newly acquainted young lady, my friend shouted, *'Matt! Run!'*

I looked to my right. Then everything went dark. Just black, nothing, a void. I was gone. Not to anywhere in particular, just nowhere. I was now in the abyss, and I would not begin to climb out until twenty-seven years later as I write this book. A hazy light came on as soon as it left; I do not know how long I was gone for. It was enough time for my friend to run and the girls to scarper. My vision was blotted and fuzzy. This was partially due to the damage that had been inflicted on me and partly due to the sticky, thick ooze that seeped from my skull.

I tried to call out, but my speech was slurred. Similar to when you're half awake and you try to scream out from a bad dream with sleep paralysis, the words just did not seem to flow from my mouth as they were screaming in my mind. Scary shit. I didn't know where I was or even for a moment who I was. I was just a beaten and torn rag doll that had been thrown aside, slumped against a wall in the street waiting for a dog to come along and piss all over him just to make things that little bit crappier.

I was so scared … fear gripped me tight. *This must be how a zombie feels when they reawaken! Am I dead?* Oh, fuck, no! *Nan!* But no words, just gibberish. *NAN!* Nothing. Then a girl appeared. She sat over me asking if I was okay. I could barely hear but could make out the words; it was as though my ears were filled with water. I struggled to stand; the feeling in my left leg and left arm had gone. After what seemed like an eternity, slowly, I pulled myself up like a zombie venturing from the grave for the first time. My face felt puffy, one eye shut; I knew my arm and leg were fucked. They felt as though they were filled with water … useless, swinging around, dangling off me as though they'd been replaced by water balloons. I tried to speak again; my voice was slurred.

I stumbled away, not knowing anything; I just had to try to move, but the pain, oh man, the pain. I felt sick all through my body, dizzy, nauseous, semi-blind, half paralyzed, and it hurt so bad, but I had to move!

Yes, make way, the walking dead has arrived in Chatham high street!

I made it around the corner, and my brother's friend found me. He took me to his mum's house. Medway Hospital was just across from his back garden behind the war memorial known as the Great Lines. I headed there. The feeling in my left leg started to come back, but my left arm and hand just hung there like a sad, deflated blow-up doll that had seen better days. Dead weight. It was a strange sensation; you could have driven a hot poker into my arm and I wouldn't have felt a thing.

I don't recall much from this point until I was in the hospital. The notorious Medway Hospital! As kids, we joked that you go in with a cold, come out in a body bag. Sadly, the joke nearly became a reality for me that day. I was in the A&E, and I remember trying to put across to the nurses how I was feeling, but, of course, I still had no idea what had happened to me. This was the time before mobile phones, so I had no way of contacting my grandparents.

My speech was improving but was still all over the place, like a drunken man pleading with his wife to listen to him. I was trying to reason with the nurse but to no avail. Oddly, what they did was put my arm in plaster, but I had no X-ray. Weird! That one still puzzles me to this day. I do remember trying to say 'My arm's not broken! It doesn't hurt!' And the nurse was just like, 'There, there, okay.' I mean, what the fuck! *Why are you not listening to me?*

They cleaned the blood off my head and my vision improved in one eye; the other was closed due to the swelling. I kept trying to say 'My arm's not broken; it feels like it's filled with water.' Then I remember the doctor and nurse talking; I could kind of hear them saying they couldn't get any sense out of me, probably drugs, and they were going to send me on my way! Shame on them. There I was, scared, alone, confused, and now disbelieved. A fine example of judgement and misunderstanding at its very best. Deduced by the National Health Service's finest. But a miracle did happen.

A man came in with an air of wisdom about him, possibly a consultant or a professor. He seemed to be walking around the hospital, maybe doing some rounds, I don't know. What I do know is that he stopped by my cubicle and greeted the nurse and doctor; they talked amongst themselves, then his voice raised and I heard him say 'Why has this boy not had a scan?' He sounded pissed off, which filled me with a little hope. Finally someone on my side.

The next sequence of events seemed to happen quickly. I was rushed in for a brain scan, then blue-lighted up to the Maudsley Hospital in London with my nan and granddad now with me. That man was the first of many people who saved my life. I will be forever grateful. The next thing I remember was sitting in intensive care with my nan and granddad, possibly also my uncle, but I'm unsure. There were a few other beds, lots of machines, and all the other patients were unconscious.

Doctor King came in; Stephen King (yes, that was his name; I will never forget, as he is also one of my favourite authors). I stood next to him and he showed me my brain scans. I had a blood clot the size of a child's fist pressing against my brain and a fractured skull. I will never forget this next moment, and I often wonder if he remembers. Doctor King looked at me and said, 'I have never had this happen before.' 'What?' I responded. 'By rights, you should be unconscious or in a coma, yet here you are, standing next to me looking at your own brain scans. This is a first for me, Matthew.' He looked at me quite emotionally. I think that was when it hit me. *I am lucky to be alive.*

They prepared me for theatre, and the following morning, as the sun came up, I had a seven-hour brain operation. I woke up. The doctor was standing beside my bed, and my nan and granddad were also there. Dr King said, 'Matthew, how do you feel?' I just gave him the thumbs up. I was alive.

What happened outside the cinema on that day? Well, it turned out that I was attacked from behind by someone using a snooker ball in a carrier bag like a makeshift mace. I assume I was struck three times, as I now have three large dents in my skull, although I feel I was more battered than struck – I also have a lot of smaller dents. But I really do not know.

Why did they attack me? Apparently, there were two of them, aged eighteen and nineteen. They had been watching the film *Scum*. The film made them excited, and they wanted to reenact the famous snooker ball in a sock scene. Bless them, budding little actors.

I was thirteen years old; the prosecution dropped the charges of attempted murder. I think GBH or ABH was what they got, and their punishment was 180 hours of community service. I got many years of pain, hurt, and darkness through addiction, fear, and anger. They got community service. Whatever it was, to me it will always be attempted murder, but however you look at it, you cannot deny it was … SAVAGE.

5. Lost

The definition of lost according to the *Collins English Dictionary*:

If you are lost or if you get lost, you do not know where you are or are unable to find your way.

I WAS ALIVE!

I can't remember how long I was in the hospital, but it was a strange time for me. I had a pipe coming out of my skull to drain the blood clot, which emptied into a bag, half my face was swollen, and I had a foot-long scar running across my head like a disused railroad for fleas. My bladder was like a football, and it hurt so bad.

I remember they wanted to put a catheter in to help me go to the toilet. That really bothered me. I was dead against this. Although the pain in my bladder was becoming unbearable, I cried, begging them not to.

For some strange reason, the thought of having a pipe inserted into my winkle was far more devastating than the one coming out of my skull. But my mind was so all over the place, I just wasn't letting them do it. Dr King said, 'Come on, Matthew, I'll take you to the toilet.' Within a few hours of my brain operation, the man who did surgery on me supported me and carried the bag of blood as I walked steadily to the toilet. Another first for him was that he helped me while I used the urinal, which was better than the alternative. Ahhh, sweet relief.

Please just give me a moment for a brief flashback to help you understand some of the other factors surrounding these events. In the years leading up to this devastating time, when I was about eleven, my brother David was in a car crash. He broke his back and was in a wheelchair. (This led to his heroin addiction later in life.) On their way back from visiting him, my nan and granddad got hit by a car driving the wrong way up a one-way street.

I know we could possibly be held responsible for crippling the NHS.

My nan broke her back and fractured her skull; my granddad lost his kneecap and the nerves in his arm. My dad was in the back and suffered minor injuries. My Uncle Pat stepped up and cared for me while also being a rock for my nan and granddad. Honestly, I must mention that if it wasn't for Pat, I don't know where I'd be now.

They were all in hospital simultaneously, and just as they all started to recover, *bang*, the snooker ball boy gets downed! You couldn't make it up; often, it felt as though we were cursed. My poor nan.

My nan and granddad were by my bedside throughout, and Pat was great at that time. In fact, everyone was; I must say I don't remember my dad being present, but that was the case throughout my entire life. One thing is for sure, our family had become a walking train wreck.

Slowly I did get on the mend. The feeling in my left arm and hand gradually started to come back, and I could steadily get up and about again. Although my left hand never returned to 100 per cent, it's only noticeable to me these days; it seems fine to the outside world. I received many cards from strangers and well-wishers after they read about me in the press and saw the TV news report.

I was improving. The pipe came out of my head, which was one of the most bizarre sensations I have ever felt. As they slowly slid it out of my skull, I felt kinda funky. I was on the mend.

They moved me back to the Medway Hospital to recover, and it wasn't long before the Predator came on hand to show his support and 'care' for me. As my body got better, though, my mental state darkened. I started to draw dark images focusing on death and write melancholy poetry to fill my days. The music I listened to on my Walkman was the same – very dark, angry, or depressing tunes. The Predator would visit and sit by the bed, stroking my leg and thigh while talking to my family and nurses.

Yeah, you know what's coming; get well soon, Matt!

Such a lovely man! YUK … VILE … MONSTER!

I felt caged within my own mind, and I started to rebel against the cage with my behaviour once I was released from the hospital. They hooked me up with a psychologist at Manor House in Gillingham, and I remember talking to him for long periods. We would discuss my thoughts and feelings, but when I felt I was beginning to open up too much, I would simply lie. Just to get out of there.

But one day in particular that always stayed with me was when he asked, 'Where do you feel happiest, Matthew?'

'When I am alone, on a hill or outside somewhere,' I replied. 'Everywhere else just seems dark, like I can't breathe.'

'Have you ever been rock climbing?'

Now, this was something that excited me! The thought of being on my own climbing up a cliff, mountain, or rock was something I felt I could find happiness doing. I wanted to try this, get out there, away from Medway, and just be alone with the wind and the birds. But we had no money, and yes, I lived in Medway; there was nowhere for me to begin this kind of sport and no one to teach me. I was deflated. Then the Predator stepped in. Oh, the hero and his white horse had arrived with a solution for my happiness and wellbeing. Once I was physically able and safe to do so, he booked me on a course with the youth hostels. I had a way to do something that would make me happy … but at what cost?

A very high one, it would seem. The rock-climbing excursions simply became covers for taking me away and incapacitating me with drugs and alcohol before raping me. Weekend after weekend, different places. I remember he bought a book with maps of climbing locations. Many were in the middle of nowhere, perfect for him, and I said nothing.

When he picked me up, there would be a can of lighter gas waiting for me in the glove box. I would reach for it as soon as we turned the corner; sometimes, if I was completely out of it, he would pull into a lay-by and sexually assault me before we had even arrived. This was, in my mind, a mixture of reality and hallucination. Until I came round midway, head aching, body sore, sometimes with vomit on my clothes, and I did not say a word. I just went in my mind to the top of a mountain somewhere – anywhere but there. I felt ashamed for years. I knew what he was doing, but I said nothing.

What the fuck, Matt? Why did you not speak? *Am I weak? Cowardly? Maybe I'm gay?* These were thoughts that entered my mind. Perhaps I just didn't care much for life anymore. Everything was dark; I didn't know who I was or where I was going, damaged and limp, just someone's rag doll they played with before tossing aside. I was *lost*.

I had recently overcome brain surgery and was being given lighter gas to inhale, vodka on tap, and sexually assaulted at the hands of the Predator and occasionally others. Sometimes he hired prostitutes; they would arrive when I was off my face and he would watch me have sex with them before he cleaned up. Where the fuck was their moral compass? One time I woke up blindfolded, velvet ties around my wrists, someone's hands on my ankles, someone else on me, and there were other voices, other older men I hadn't heard before. It was a haze, a painful haze. The following day nothing was said, and although I was sore, I just behaved as though nothing had happened. What happens on the road trip … stays on the road trip. That was how I began to view things.

Another dark episode was when he went through a phase of making videos. In the videos, I talked to the camera about dying. I remember when I even made a video for my nan and granddad just in case I did die. Like a farewell. While he sat in the background watching as he emptied his bag of tricks. I even discussed with him how I would kill myself. I wish I had those tapes now; although not easy watching, I am sure they would give insight into a cry for help from a damaged child that no one could see. I think he got off on this, the video-making phase. But I never spoke out.

In everyone's eyes, this man was helping me, but in fact he was burying me, and this is the thing about the cunning and manipulative prowess of the paedophile. I learnt through my years of being sexually assaulted by that man that he was so convincing to the outside world, and he had no empathy for the child – how could he? I was half dead and brain-damaged. Any one of those nights, I might not have woken up. Then what? Now I look back and I can't see how the hell it happened, and no one realised, and I didn't speak out. But it did happen, and now I am speaking out.

With my inner world crumbling, I started to lash out. A regular school couldn't put up with me anymore, so I went to hospital school due to my anger management issues. The day I threw a knife at my CDT teacher was the day school pretty much ended for me. However, I could go one day a week, you know, just to keep my finger in.

What the school did do for me was to send me on a thing called the youth award scheme, where I went to work with an electrician a couple of days a week. The other days were hospital school and, if I could be bothered, one day at regular school. My schooling, at this point, was pretty much over. I had become unruly at home, and my solvent abuse was increasing. I started inhaling deodorants, furniture polish, and hairspray (a particular favourite). My nan got wise; my face was filled with spots and my eyes looked empty. I started finding leaflets about solvent abuse around the house. I remember one night, in particular, we had an argument. I can't remember what it was about. Still, I do remember that I tried to kill myself by repeatedly smashing my head against my bedroom wall till blood poured down my face, completely out of control and on a one-way road to oblivion. My nan had to call Helen out (the social worker from hospital school) to calm me down.

And still I said nothing. Inside, I was falling apart. The quiet little boy from Medway was turning a new, more devastating corner. I went on the attack, paranoid of everyone I met and worried that I would be attacked again. I began striking people. I would hit first, ask later, which got me in trouble with the police on several occasions. I started to enjoy violence. Maybe now I was living up to my father's standards! No, these are things I am not proud of, and to this day feel guilty about the damage I caused and the unnecessary pain I inflicted when I decided to smash someone up just for looking at me.

In many ways, I was becoming my father, though, a bully ... but a bully because I was too scared to speak up. If the truth be known, inside, I was crying, a little boy torn apart, but to the world, I put on a front, which went on for years. I was arrested for violent disorder, causing affray, criminal damage, ABH, attempted theft, theft, assault, and possession, all before I was eighteen. The only reason I never went to jail was because of the psychological reports regarding my brain injury.

I lacked empathy for other people, compassion for my family, and kindness for myself. My entire demeanour had changed. I wore black clothes, listened to dark music, and went away on excursions knowing I would be the centre of someone's depravity. Still, I didn't care at this point as long as he supplied me with the means I needed to escape.

Vodka, solvents, poppers, weed, whatever. I didn't care what it was as long as it did the trick.

I was spiralling. I didn't care anymore. *Do what you want with my body as long as you give me what I need.*

The little boy who always wanted to fly was gone, and an addict was born.

When I was eighteen, I joined the army and served as a Pioneer. By this time, my abuser had stopped sexually abusing me. However, I still felt some kind of loyalty towards him. I remember I saw him on the park and told him I was signing up. That was the day I finally broke away from him. When I met him at the park and told him I was joining the armed forces, he started crying.

I consoled him; I know this may be hard to understand, but I did. I still felt at that moment as though he had been some kind of father figure to me. I know that sounds insane, but I pitied him while also feeling like I was closing a chapter of my life. The pain he had put me through and the sickening ordeals like filming farewell videos to my nan as if I had died. Being under the influence or regaining consciousness to find myself being held down by one man and used by another. Not quite knowing how many people were actually in the room, but allowing myself to be taken away in my mind to another place.

It was not at the forefront of my mind; it was buried deep within. But now, looking back, I know why he was crying. It was fear. He knew I would find my strength one day, and he knew at that moment that I was not that little boy anymore.

He was scared. Shortly after I joined up, he killed himself. But I never managed to close that chapter and I never got to see him punished in a court of law. I never got to speak out.

He had won that battle. I continued to turn to alcohol and drugs for comfort to forget and self-medicate. This was a major blow to me, as was the conviction of the men who had nearly killed me. A hundred and eighty hours of community service was an unsatisfactory punishment for almost taking my life. Almost killing me in a savage, unprovoked attack when I was just thirteen years old. Within myself, I felt I must be worth very little to the world, so I continued to push the self-destruct button.

6. There Are Wolves amidst the Sheep

They say the greatest trick the devil ever did was convincing the world he did not exist. This is how I have come to look at those who seek to groom our children through deceit and cunning. In many ways, the child groomer is the devil himself, stalking the Earth and devouring the light from the life and innocence that they encounter. A very real and dangerous character walks among us; a wolf amidst the sheep. I want to take a moment to share with you my thoughts on these predators and how we can combat them.

As someone who was sexually abused as a child, I feel that this taboo subject is one of the biggest threats to our young, and through awareness, we can halt the abusers' plans before it is too late. When a sexual predator targets their prey, in many cases, but not all, they are prepared for the long game. In fact, the thrill of the hunt could almost be equal to the deed itself as their fantasies build and anticipation drives them.

When I was being groomed as a child, it was done over the course of a long time. It felt like months and could even have been a year or so before I was initially sexually assaulted. This lengthy process was necessary for my abuser to gain my trust and, more importantly, that of my family members.

This was a risky business for him, as I came from a very tough family known for being violent. However, I believe I was targeted because we did not have much money. My father wasn't around much, and my granddad was away at sea. My abuser used to stop and talk to me when I was playing out the front on my own, and he struck up a friendship with my nan, just in passing, letting us know he worked for the police – a perfect cover.

There was no need to worry about stranger danger, as his mum was a neighbour, and back then, the word paedophile wasn't heard of; we were just told to stay away from stereotypical dirty old men. This guy wasn't dirty; he had money, he worked for the police, and his mum was a neighbour.

He spent time building confidence and casting his shadow over our trusted world like cancer, unnoticeable and easily missed until it's too late.

After I was raped for the first time, I knew something was wrong. Although my mind was hazy and unclear due to the alcohol, I was still innocent then. He passed off the pain in my body, the bleeding and soreness, as me falling when I was drunk. This monster made me feel as though he was looking out for me. I wouldn't get in trouble for being pissed if I kept quiet.

As time went on and I became more aware, I didn't feel I could talk to my nan or granddad or my dad. The sexual assaults got worse, with other men being involved as time went on. So did the plying of alcohol and substances, which in time became a form of self-medication and escape. Still, I was unaware that that was what I was doing at the time.

Alongside the sexual abuse, the psychological wearing down was also continuous. Talking about suicide, making videos for my family as if I had topped myself. I often think I am lucky to be alive. Was one of these videos made to make it look like I had killed myself? Looking back, it was like being a hostage in plain sight.

As a parent, it's natural to think about these things and how I can protect my children, especially in today's world of games consoles, mobile phones, the internet, and other technologies. We are more connected than we have ever been, but I fear there is a genuine danger of becoming more disconnected from our children as the days go by. It was not my family's fault that I felt I could not talk to them, as the way I was raised was the only way they knew how, and my nan did the very best she could with the knowledge she had.

That's why it is important to me that we encourage each other, as a species, to talk, to communicate, in the real world. We can see and feel others' emotions. By learning to understand without casting judgement, we open our arms to our kids and other people who need to reach out, who need to be heard but cannot find the words.

In all honesty, if we can take the time to really know one another, often words are not needed.

If I had felt I could speak up without shame, without feeling like I had done wrong or that I would be judged or punished, if I had dared to say 'That man did this to me' ... then the sexual abuse would have stopped. But instead, it got worse and harder for me to climb out of the abyss until eventually, I was pulled under.

And although I survived, I didn't begin to climb out of the darkness until I was forty years old, when this journey of my recovery began. We need to actively listen to our children without shutting them down, without being an authority that imposes on them with judgmental eyes and a firm hand. We must stay connected to our young people to spot the signs of when they are unhappy within themselves and not put everything down to teenage angst.

We need to ask them how they feel, be open and honest with them as we hope they will be with us. Some people are happy when their kids are in their rooms, quiet, because they are out of the way and they can carry on adulting in peace.

When my boy is quiet, I go into his room and say 'Hey, Buster, you okay? How was school today?' When he answers me, I try to actively listen and engage, but it's not always what he says that shows me how he's feeling … it's what he isn't saying that I don't want to miss.

We need to spend time with our kids and engage with them without silencing them. As a kid, I heard the phrase 'children should be seen and not heard' a lot. I believe we should be encouraging them to have a voice. Allowing that voice to be heard, or, more importantly, showing them that it is listened to without fear of reprisal, is the greatest weapon we have for protection against predators.

Parenting is hard, and unfortunately, our kids don't come with a manual. But by listening and communicating with them and letting them know that they do have a voice while making them aware of the genuine dangers that are out there, we are making a good start.

As a parent, I haven't always been present; I've been a barker and not a listener in the past. But I will say with a sober mind and an understanding of what happened to me that I would never want anything like that for my children – like most parents. I will try my hardest to be more present, more open, and more attentive to what's going on in my kids' lives and within themselves as best as I can.

7. Joseph

There are no words I can find in the dictionary to define my son or the pain I felt with his loss.

My ex-wife and I were separated when we found out she was pregnant with Joseph. I promised I would stop drinking and support her as a husband should. At the twelve-week scan, we were told that we had to go to St Mary's Hospital in London because there were concerns regarding our baby's development. There could be a chance of spina bifida, a birth defect that occurs when the spine and spinal cord don't form properly. We were distraught and incredibly nervous about the appointment. Still, we decided that this was our child, and we would love and care for them no matter what the doctors said … there is always hope. The news was to be far worse.

My son was diagnosed with anencephaly. Anencephaly is the absence of a significant portion of the brain, skull, and scalp that develops during the embryonic stage. The doctors told us that the chances of survival outside of the womb were nil, with the most prolonged recorded survival of a baby with anencephaly being just twenty-eight months. However, most children with anencephaly die during birth or shortly afterwards.

Heartbroken, devastated, and momentarily disengaged from the world, everything came crashing down. I had never felt darkness encase me quite like this before, and I hope never to again. Our options were discussed: either abortion or for my ex-wife to carry Joseph like a normal pregnancy and give birth. Being a strong Catholic, I knew she would not want an abortion, and I guess I didn't expect her to. A mother wants the best for her child, and I suppose there was always a chance that he would survive ... there is always hope.

She told me that she would like to give him whatever life she could, even if it was for a short period while in her womb, and I understand that. Still struggling with my own demons, I was not stable enough to be the man I needed to be. The next nine months were the most challenging nine months of my life. I could not handle feeling my son kick, move, and grow in my ex-wife's womb with the thought in the back of my mind that I would never see him grow up, and this tore me apart.

This was pain like none other. I cannot explain it, feeling your baby grow, talking to him in the womb, knowing he will die. I know it destroyed her too, and any other man would have stepped up to the plate, but I didn't ... I couldn't.

I selfishly continued to turn to alcohol and drugs for support, self-medicating the only way I knew how. Everyone seemed concerned about my ex-wife's feelings, and I felt very much out of the loop and unable to cope, trapped within my own mind, feeling like my life was a cycle of continuous hurt and pain.

This made things worse for her, I know, but at the time, I could not see beyond my own tears and pain. For that, I will forever be genuinely sorry. In her eyes, as well as those of her family, I was a no-good alcoholic scumbag. I accept that and hold my hands up. If I saw another man behaving that way, I would view him with disgust, but that man is me. I have to view him with disgust every time I see his reflection and whenever I close my eyes, replaying the events of the past.

When she gave birth to Joseph, I was there. He was born, and the top of his skull had not formed. My beautiful boy. I held him in my arms for a few minutes as he passed away, and something inside me died too.

The arguments with my ex were ferocious, as she had stopped me from seeing my daughter. I could only see things from my own perspective. Perhaps if I had been able to see things from hers, I could have understood, but I didn't. What broke me was the day of his funeral. I carried his little coffin into the church. I was now living in Kent with my nan; I drove up to London alone for the funeral. After the funeral, there was a small get-together at my ex's mum's house.

I went there, and my daughter came running down the path. 'Daddy!' she shouted as I picked her up and swung her in the air. This was what I needed, my little girl giving her dad a big hug. A moment of healing … but it wasn't to last. My ex came out and said, 'What are you doing here?'

To my astonishment, I replied, 'It's my son's funeral.'

Very coldly, the response I got was 'You're not welcome here.' I was like, 'What?' She said, 'Don't cause a scene, just go.'

I looked at my daughter and just fell apart. I got in my car and cried all the way back to Kent; the pain was unbearable. Looking back now, I don't blame her one bit, as she was hurting too, but I could not understand this at the time. That was the day my gateway into addiction became firmly locked into place, and I allowed it to consume me.

Over the years, I became a master of manipulation, cunning, and creativity in my hunt for alcohol and drugs. Very few people knew the extent of my consumption.

I didn't care about anything except having a can of cider in my hand and smokes in my pocket. If the option appeared, MDMA was my drug of choice, or cocaine. A bottle of white spirit would probably have appealed to me. I lost my job. I was made redundant the day after my son died. I lost my family and moved from bedsit to bedsit until I eventually ended up back at my nan's. When I was alone at night, I went through huge bouts of paranoia, which got me into several violent altercations.

One night, I could hear banging in the bedsit underneath me, where a couple of guys were staying. With my frame of mind not being as it should, I thought they were trying to 'get' me. Every time I moved, there was a bang. This got so bad that one night I found myself sitting up in the corner, getting as tight in as I could, shaking but desperately trying not to move for fear.

Eventually, after several hours, I exploded and burst into the other extreme. Grabbing a bar I had been clenching, I burst into their place and attacked like a crazed animal.

I had become something else; I look back now, and that was not me that night. It is as though I was taken over by something other than me, because everything now seems like an out-of-body experience. But at the end of the day, it happened; I must own it.

I left and went to stay with my friends. They were very good to me – took me in and looked after me when I was at my lowest. The alcohol and the drugs were steadily growing into an all day, everyday occurrence. I eventually left and made my way back to my nan's. Often, I would spend my time just wandering around fields with no purpose or direction.

Other days, sitting in the dark with the hours tick-tocking away, I could easily have allowed myself to sink deeper into the abyss.

When I look back on those days, I remember sniffing coke off the carpet that I thought someone may have spilt – actually licking it at one point. Waking up on a roundabout in the middle of a busy road in London during rush hour. Finding myself handcuffed to a radiator after being drugged in a stranger's flat, about to be raped. I've been through all the different emotions: shame, anger at myself, guilt, anxiety. But now, I just feel sad; my life spiralled after the loss of my son. But I still had a daughter. I couldn't get myself out of the grip of my own dark world and into the light of hers. But I accept this now. I simply couldn't cope, and my son's death tipped me over the edge. I don't think anyone in my life saw it coming or its extent.

I never talked about the pain I felt; I tried to mask it because I couldn't see what was happening to me. I was simply drifting.

8. Where Was My Worth?

As I got older, I was always drug and alcohol hungry. I would drink with hollow legs, eat ecstasy tablets like they were smarties, and lick granules of cocaine off the floor to ensure I would get as much as possible, and still, I would want more.

Even at a very young age, in my early teens, my nan could not keep aerosol cans in the house because once I finished off lighter fluid, I would inhale hairspray, deodorant, furniture polish, and air freshener. Basically, if it was an aerosol, I would use it. I would spray it through a tea towel directly into my mouth to inhale it; lighter fluid like red band gas I would simply spray between my teeth directly into my mouth and throat. Direct to the lungs via the throat. My nan would find empty cans and the corners of tea towels or rags, lavender fresh, hidden in my room or around the house.

When I inhaled, I knew the dangers, as my nan kept leaving pamphlets about solvent abuse lying around. When I took stimulants such as cocaine or ecstasy, I would not stop until all was gone. And alcohol … well, I would drink until I passed out. All on a regular, often daily, basis. Looking back now with a sober, honest viewpoint, this was never fun, even in my early teens. This was an escape, and if the escape led to death, I really didn't care, as long as I was gone in my mind and gone in my heart. I am fortunate to be alive.

I was never consciously aware that I was masking pain and suppressing my emotions. This was simply an automatic response to my inward need for healing that I never received. The mind can be a battlefield where the heart fears to tread. I was, in many ways, defeated before my life had begun. I spent many hours trapped within myself, tormented by the scenes of sexual depravity I had survived, along with the thought that my life had nearly been taken from me so savagely. Where was my worth? Deep within, I felt as though I had none, and that is how I progressed for many years.

9. Sharon and Me

I met Sharon and her two children, Bryce and Savannah, after I had moved back to Kent and was living with my nan in June 2009. She was like a breath of fresh air – kind, compassionate, and so easy-going. I was still drinking heavily and taking drugs, although I drank more than I took drugs and managed to pass it off as being a social, fun drinker. When I met Sharon, I had taken on the persona of a free-living hippy type, loving life, carefree, and trying to find my way. There was an instant attraction, and I knew I wanted to be with this woman for the rest of my life.

We made a fantastic couple, and my family accepted Bryce and Savannah as their own. To the outside world, all was fantastic, and in many ways it was, but, truth be told, what I really needed was healing. I just couldn't see this, or I wasn't really open to it. I will say here that I don't think my and Sharon's paths crossed by chance. I believe that meeting her was an integral part of my life's journey, but at that time and for many years afterwards, I couldn't see how important she was to me.

Drinking daily, I gave up the drugs off my own bat, but I was drinking more and skillfully hiding it behind my fun, hippy façade. Being with Sharon opened new doors to me, and I learnt so much. Sharon was a spiritual healer. She taught me a great deal regarding meditation and healing ourselves on an energetic level. She showed me compassion, empathy, and unconditional love.

I became very interested in Buddhist teachings about mindfulness and other practices such as shamanism. I had always had a deep love of the outdoors and spending time with nature. I saw books on shamanism when I was married, and it had always interested me. Still, due to my ex-wife's Catholic beliefs, I had never looked into it. Sharon encouraged me to delve into spiritual practices and taught me meditation.

I enjoyed this and learnt as much as I could about different spiritual practices. I found that, over time, I built a new mask, a new persona, when instead I could have been using this invaluable knowledge to help myself heal from my past.

I became fixated on learning spiritual practices during the day and drinking, often secretly, at night. I thought I had found a balance, but I wasn't really practising these skills at all; I was instead using them to fuel my own ego. I couldn't hold a job down for long due to my stubbornness and short temper. I would walk out while ranting and raving 'I'm not doing that, fuck this' and other excuses or reasons. Sharon always accepted and put up with it.

She always supported me no matter what, and I often think that one trait I received from my mum – if what my nan told me is true – is that I am never happy.

I could never settle down and be content with my lot. The minute I settled and things started to go well, I would hover my finger over the self-destruct button, allowing the whirlpool of addiction to storm in and begin to bury me once more. Looking back, I often think that it is during the times when things start to go well and the calmer days come that I am forced to hold a mirror up to myself and my journey. When the fear sets in, the memories come back, and I always struggled to cope. I struggled to accept myself and move forward. Inwardly, I still felt shame and as though I did not deserve to be happy.

I know I pushed Sharon to the brink of despair often, but she never showed that to me, or perhaps I was too selfish to see it. I mistreated her at times over the years. I wanted us to have a good life. Still, I was never prepared to do anything more than think about five o'clock in the afternoon. My excuses could start for why I needed a drink, and so the wheels continued to turn.

No holidays; days out became less and less. We both worked, but we never had any money, as I would just spunk it all on alcohol or nonsense. I was always coming up with ideas for businesses or websites. I would start them but would never have the consistency to keep them going or build them into anything worthwhile. At one point, we even had a shop. Still, I was more interested in the shop being a place where I could be the big I am rather than working hard and turning it into the family business I had promised.

I could never build a solid foundation for anything. This was largely because of alcohol. I continued to drown myself using this poison because the finger wouldn't come away from the self-destruct button. The shop failed because I kept giving stuff away, and that was it, plain and simple. The shop failed because I didn't do the groundwork. It failed because, deep down, subconsciously, I didn't really think I deserved anything worthwhile. I didn't have the consistency to see my hopes and dreams through to fruition; it was far easier to have a quick fix of alcohol and continue on the carousel.

At one point, I was having addicts come into the shop wanting to make a couple of quid, and I would buy their old crap off them when I had no money in the pot to feed my own family. But Sharon stood by me and did not give up on me, supporting my every decision and picking me up every single time I fell on my arse. I had a second chance when Tyler was born. My world lit up completely. At the time, I was going to court with my ex to see my daughter. It is a long and arduous process, as I'm sure you can imagine, that involved social workers and reports for this and that. I was accused of everything from domestic violence to being the addict that, in fact, I was.

So when Sharon told me she was pregnant with Tyler, I was so happy but at the same time incredibly worried, as the memories of losing Joseph were still so strong. I didn't think I could handle losing another child, which would really push me over the edge. I thank my lucky stars each day that Tyler came into the world a happy, healthy baby. For many, this would have been the time to step up and be the man they needed to be. And in many ways, I do think I did. Tyler and I have an incredible bond. He knows he is loved, and I did try to make up for many of my mistakes.

But on the other hand, I continued on the same carousel of drinking and self-punishment, which had a knock-on effect on my little family.

We moved house three times in as many years, and when my old boss asked me if I would consider moving up to Burton-on-Trent, I jumped at the chance. I had pretty much run out of options in Medway in regard to job prospects, and I thought maybe I could make a fresh start. Everything would be great. Sharon never questioned this; she agreed to move away from what she knew, her friends, family, and everything, to support me.

Looking back now, I realise how selfish I was. Yes, this was an excellent move for me. Still, did I really take my family's feelings into account? Was I simply being my usual self-centred self and following my hopes and dreams without considering hers?

I always thought I knew what was best, but I didn't. We moved and I continued; in fact, in many ways, I got worse. I had moved Sharon away from the life she knew. I had relocated myself further away from my daughter, yet I hadn't escaped my need to self-medicate; I hadn't beaten the demons of my past. They followed me. Nothing changed.

I wasn't in a good place. I felt completely disjointed from myself, my family, and the world around me. I had to get away, be alone. I felt as though I simply wanted to break away and allow my addictions to take over. This was a pivotal time for me. I told Sharon I had to get away and sort myself out, but deep down, my intention was not to fix myself. I intended to push that button and allow myself to sink into the abyss. My thoughts were not with what was best for my family. I didn't care about the effect I would have on other people. I was focused on myself because I felt like I was caged, and the cage was getting smaller each day.

Could it have been depression? Maybe a midlife crisis or some kind of breakdown? I do not know, because although Sharon had told me before that I should seek therapy, I did not. I was weak at that point, and I moved out of our family home, breaking my sons' hearts and leaving Sharon high and dry. I just could not see beyond my own desire to be free to drink what I wanted, when I wanted, away from the eyes of those who loved me. I know it sounds like madness, and I am not painting myself in a very good light, but that is how it was.

I rented a furnished one-bedroom flat about five miles away. I still went to work, and of an evening, my alcohol consumption was peaking. I was also smoking weed again. I would buy twelve cans of premium lager and a bottle of wine on my way home. I would have the wine when I first got home – the highest percentage of red wine I could buy – and it went down fast. Then I would start on the lagers. I basically drank to blackout daily. I was hardly eating, or if I was eating, it was just crisps and other crap. Every evening I was getting to the point where I would argue with Sharon and my vicious forked tongue would strike out with its verbal assaults.

One night I actually drove over to the house and showed her up in front of everyone on the street, throwing empty beer cans at the front door. I can't remember how I got home that night, but thank God I did, and I didn't hurt anyone. What was wrong with me? I felt so alone, yet I didn't need to be! I put myself in that situation and gave up on life, family, everything. I had it all and was ready to throw it away once again. This was not an ordinary person's actions; I broke inside while destroying my outside world.

Then, one night, the phone rang. 'Matt, Nan's going downhill; we don't think she will be with us much longer. You need to get down here.' My nan had been diagnosed with vascular dementia some years before and was living in a care home. I had only seen her a couple of times since I'd moved to Burton, again something I deeply regret and will have to live with.

I had to go see her before the inevitable happened. Growing up in Medway, my nan was my mum. She had always done her best by me, and here she was now, dying in a home. In many ways, I felt as though I had failed her by moving away. The thing is, we never realise that one day will be the last day we see those we love. We take people for granted until it's too late. My nan first started getting sick after my granddad passed away. I had stayed with him the night he left us, and I had to go see my nan and let her know I was there.

I told my boss I needed a few days off and went to Colchester. Seeing my nan like that broke my heart. We were now in the first lockdown. We had to wear full PPE, and I sat with her holding her hand with my uncle and auntie present. She seemed to drift in and out of consciousness. I held her hand, and I know in my heart that she knew I was there. She tried to talk a couple of times, but the words did not come out. I looked into her eyes and could see her tears; she looked scared, and I felt useless. I drove back to Burton, as there were no hotels and I couldn't stay at the home due to covid. I planned to go back the following day. I was about to leave when my auntie phoned me and told me my nan had passed.

Everything came crashing down in that instant. I know we knew it was coming, but it hits you like a ton of bricks when it does. Memories of my nan were rampaging through my mind, along with the guilt of not being there for her, not being able to do anything to help her. The fact that I had been more interested in myself than in making an effort to go see her plagued my mind. This catapulted me into a week or so of burying myself within an alcoholic mess. I listened to sad music of an evening and drank myself into a stupor. People kept phoning me to make sure I was okay, but I didn't want to listen. I wasn't interested. I wasn't eating; all I wanted to do was get smashed, and I got nasty when I did. I would wake up, tidy the flat, clear up all the remnants from the night before, go and visit Tyler, then repeat the previous night's actions, sit alone, and get off my face.

Sharon struggled with the first lockdown, and I just didn't care. I am so ashamed of myself now, but all I thought about was my alcoholic pity party and me. This went on until the funeral. Things were now set in stone, and I felt ready to embrace the darkness and be what I felt others thought I always had been. A scumbag drunk.

Then something happened. The morning after the funeral, I woke up hungover and felt extremely sorry for myself. I had no motivation to move and just curled up in my pit with tears streaming down my face. My heart was heavy and my mind felt like a foggy wasteland, unclear and unable to focus. All I could picture was my nan lying there helpless, scared, and there was nothing I could do. My granddad was gone, now my nan – the end of an era.

I couldn't, I didn't want to move. What was the point? I had never felt so alone as I did in that moment. Even though my nan had been poorly for quite some time, I still always took comfort in the fact that she was still around. Now the certainty of never hearing her voice again was so overwhelming, I felt at a loss.

As I lay there, the thoughts about my nan kept spinning around my mind, combined with fear and an intense sensation of anxiety. 'I'm so sorry, Nan,' I said, hoping she could hear me. I could hear her in my mind responding, 'Come on, Matthew, get yourself up. There's no point lying there; come on.' Then I remembered a sentence she said to me often when she was alive.

'When I die, don't use me as an excuse to get drunk.'

My nan hated alcohol; in her eyes, it had always been the ruin of her boys. She despised drinking, and I know she couldn't stand that the first thing we did was turn to the bottle whenever we had a problem.

Those words were now stuck on a loop, taking over my internal monologue.

'Matthew, don't use me as an excuse to get drunk.'

Half the day had gone when I finally found the nerve to got up and use the toilet. When I did, it was hard to escape looking in the mirror and being greeted by bloodshot eyes combined with the feeling of tightness around my head. I had become so accustomed to this over the years, alongside the continuous *thud, thud, thud* pounding away at the inside of my skull like a demon determined to escape its bony cage.

I threw my head over the toilet bowl and retched, feeling my insides tearing apart and making my breathing shallow and harsh. When I came up and thought I could breathe again, I looked in the mirror at my red puffy stare. I could see my dad looking back at me. I knew that look – the face of an alcoholic.

Then her voice came again. 'Don't use me as an excuse to get drunk.'

That's it, I need to change. I have to. I'm never drinking again, I proclaimed to myself. But how? *Clean up, Matt; first, clean up.* I looked around my front room. Cans and bottles all over the coffee table. I grabbed a bin bag and began clearing up. It was so warm; I had that sticky feeling when the alcohol seems to seep out of every pore. I went to the fridge and grabbed a carton of orange juice and started guzzling it like it was my first pint of the evening. I was so dehydrated that it felt good. *Okay, right, shower time.* I was on one now. *Get cleaned up. I'll feel much better.* While I was showering, the words came back again.

'When I die, don't use me as an excuse to get drunk.'

'I won't, Nan.'

I spent the rest of the day on my computer researching alcoholism and addiction. I knew that it was recommended that you visit your GP (and if you are embarking on your own recovery journey, I cannot impress enough the importance of getting yourself checked out before you pack in the booze) and join a local support group. Still, we were in a lockdown, so that wasn't going to happen.

So I started looking for other suggestions and I came across some information stating that journaling would help you try to give up an addiction. Many people have found that keeping a video journal is even better because talking to the camera is a bit like talking to a therapist. You're getting things off your chest, expressing how you feel. Sharon had always said I needed therapy, but with my job and the long hours I work, that never seemed possible. But a video diary – I could do that. *Yes, that's it. I'll pack up alcohol, and I'll do it while keeping track of my progress as part of a video journal.*

I felt elated and focused. *Now I need a platform, a means to log my recovery videos online.* After looking around, I decided to start a Facebook page and call it Alcohol No More. Perfect. I had a plan. This was a cause for celebration, and now I was feeling much better, so I decided I'd pop to the shop, get some alcohol, and start tomorrow. So that's what I did. At five o'clock I got wasted and the rest of the night is a blur. Mission failed at the very first hurdle. *But tomorrow's a new day!*

The next day I went to work, and when I had a break, I made my first video, Day One, and uploaded it to Facebook. But I wasn't ready again, and so that night, I lapsed, slipped up, and returned to Day One. Mission failed yet again at the first hurdle. How could I not even get past one night?

'When I die, don't use me as an excuse to get drunk.'

'I'm trying, Nan, but it's so hard.'

I decided there and then that I had to get strategic and attack my problem.

After that first lapse, I felt incredibly frustrated and ashamed of myself. I thought about it all day, and I worked out that I would have to look at all areas of my lifestyle and much more if I was going to succeed this time. I concluded that I did not eat before having that first drink; when I thought about it, I never ate my evening meal at a reasonable time. I would always drink first and pick at food later after getting drunk. After that failure, I noted that I needed to try eating my evening meal before drinking alcohol. Perhaps this change in behaviour would take the edge off my cravings.

Getting vital nutrients back into our system when we go into recovery is crucial, as alcohol strips the body of all that goodness. So eating properly would be essential in gaining some back and rebuilding myself into a healthier, happier me.

Nutrition

When I was drinking heavily, I never gave a second thought to my body's needs regarding nutrition. Yet nutrition is vital for us to function correctly day to day. While amid my alcoholism, the only requirement I felt focused on was where my next drink was coming from. As I began my road to recovery, I started looking into rebuilding my body into a healthier me. Let me just point out here, I didn't set out to become a gym god or a fitness fanatic, but when I sat back and looked at my lifestyle, I came to a realisation.

While I was abusing alcohol, I didn't eat the correct amount of food to sustain me. I often skipped meals. The foods I did eat were often lacking in proper nutrients. My stomach would not absorb the nutrients my body needed due to the damage I had caused it. I would also lose nutrients by throwing up or having a runny tummy. (To put it nicely – sorry if you're eating, but let's be honest – I got the squits regularly.)

Craving proper nutrients made me feel anxious and irritable and disrupt my sleeping patterns. This, in turn, had a knock-on effect, causing me to feel tired, depressed, and unhappy. When I think about this, I often think about when I am at work. Let me give you an example. On the days at work when I hadn't drunk enough water or eaten, my mood and morale greatly affected me.

When I did eat, but it was takeaway food from the services, I was left feeling sluggish and unmotivated. When I observed myself like this and my eating habits, I began to see how important proper nutrition is, and, trust me, coupled with the problems alcohol alone was causing me, the effect on my relationships and work life was not great. Everything tied into one catastrophic mess!

I am no nutritionist, but here are my thoughts on what I felt I needed to help with my recovery.

Balance

I wanted to have some balance in my diet. I wanted to start eating more beans, lentils, peas, etc. More root vegetables such as potatoes and carrots would be tremendous, and pasta – maybe some seeded bread. I also wanted to make sure I ate adequate protein – chicken, tuna, etc. Nothing too fatty, as I don't like fat. I would include dairy as well – milk, butter, etc.

These are foods that are high in carbohydrates, which help to balance serotonin levels, a hormone that helps you to relax, as well as protein to help get me back into tip-top condition.

I also bought myself some multivitamins, which included the B vitamins – as a deficiency in these is common in alcoholism – vitamin C, zinc, magnesium, and calcium.

Eating Healthily to Build the New Me!

In the first two weeks, I felt my hunger gradually rise initially, though I ate small meals, as I simply wasn't used to the digestion process. By the end of week two, I fell into the trap of comfort eating in the evening. I know eating a bit of crap is undoubtedly better than drinking myself into oblivion; however, this would not be beneficial to me in the long term. In the first year of alcohol recovery, my nutrition needs would be far greater than usual.

To this end, I would need to try to eat a healthy balanced diet daily. I knew this could be difficult with my job, but I would have to try to maintain some consistency. I thought this could get boring, so I decided to keep my foods varied and try new things. Essentially, I was learning to try new foods and cook. This was my game plan for nutrition, and it was nice and straightforward. Cut down on sweets and sugar in general. I drink a lot of water now; I focus on maintaining my hydration. Before going into recovery, I rarely drank water on its own, but now I wouldn't be without it.

If I did feel like something nice, I opted for a high-fibre option with oats, fruit, or maybe a muffin. I also decided to start doing some light exercise, just three nights a week. Exercising makes me feel good. Improves my health. If I'm exercising, I'm not drinking, and I tell you, I certainly don't feel like a drink afterwards. In fact, exercising during my trigger times in the evening, I thought, could really help me.

10. Early Obstacles

So I decided to start eating healthier, which brought forward a new obstacle I hadn't even considered – going to the shop. Sharon always did the food shopping online, and I hadn't given it a second thought before. I tell you this, though, my friend, the shops can be a battlefield for the alcoholic who is in recovery and trying to abstain from their poison.

The first hurdle I discovered regarding this challenge was the time of day that I visited the shop. I couldn't go after work, which meant I was confronted by alcohol smack bang during my trigger time. The second hurdle I encountered was the amount of alcohol that actually takes up space in our local shops. There are more aisles given to alcoholic beverages than anything else. This is true; have a look when you're out and about. Then there was a third obstacle; due to the lockdown, they forced the queues for the tills up one or two aisles, and as I only had a basket, I was directed to the self-checkout. That queue went up the seasonal aisle, which, guess what, was filled with alcohol! I am not shitting you. Booze was everywhere I turned, and it seemed someone was testing me on that first trip.

It was incredibly hard. I just wanted to get my bits and bobs for my evening meal and lunch at work and get out. But do you know what? I was okay. I actually learnt from that trip. I knew that in future I needed to shop online or do a more extensive weekly shop on my day off in the morning when I wasn't going through my trigger time of day. Planning and preparation. As long as I could keep learning from what I experienced and adapt my typical behaviour pattern, I felt I could get through this. That day became a small victory over my addictions.

I made sure I stocked up on flavoured water. I knew that when I begin to abstain from alcohol, there was a chance I would sweat a great deal when in bed. If I have the sweats at night, it stood to reason that there was a good chance I would lose a lot of fluid, and I was already pretty dehydrated. I planned to sip water throughout the evening and also replenish it during the day.

I was dreading the night times because one of the excuses I had convinced myself of over the years was that I could not sleep without alcohol. First, because when my mind slowed down at bedtime, I would replay my childhood traumas. Second, because I was so used to drinking to blackout, normal sleep never seemed like an option. I feared the night, but I knew it was on its way, and I would have to ride it out.

One of the things that helped me get through that first evening was tuning in to one of the AA Zoom meetings online. This occupied me during that first night. I found that listening to people who had been where I was and gone on to live sober lives successfully gave me a confidence boost and an element of hope. *It can be done, Matt; if they can do it, you can do it too*, and everything I was going through, others had gone through before. Although I didn't talk on the Zoom, I didn't need to. Just listening helped me through what otherwise could have been a tough night.

It was still challenging, I guess. I only had about one hour of sleep before I had to go to work, and when I woke, my bed was drenched in sweat. It was horrible, the smell was awful, and the feeling on my skin was disgusting. Still, I knew this was coming and that over the next few days, I would be changing my bedding frequently. *This won't go on forever, Matt. You have to ride it out, buddy. You can get through this.*

With the toxins leaving my body during the day, I started to reflect on my life and ponder questions such as when my drinking began and the starting point. My recovery had become all-encompassing, and, in a way, I was glad about this. I wanted to take this seriously and felt I had to start looking at where my path had taken me if I was going to succeed.

Listening in on the AA Zoom meeting actually sparked something in me – a desire to talk about my gateways into addiction, as I described at the book's start. This was a challenging thing for me to begin to share on camera. However, I knew in my heart that if I wanted to recover correctly, I needed to open up and be honest with myself by confronting my past and talking about it. This, to me, felt like the beginning of acceptance. And through talking, I would be able to learn to let go. This was important to me, as I didn't want my children to end up living as I had and as my father and uncles did. By talking and successfully moving forward, I could break the addiction cycle that seemed to run in my family.

The Change

Throughout my life, most mornings I would get up feeling as though I needed to start a new journey or walk a new path. I knew this within myself; however, there was often something standing in my way, and once I started to develop a clear head, I could see that it was the communication between my heart and my mind that was the major obstacle.

The desires of my heart were constantly in battle with the fears and anxiety being put forward by my oh-so-chaotic mind. What my heart longed for required CHANGE, but my mind would become agitated by the thought of change and would often overpower the heart, keeping me trapped in the cycle of addiction, pain, and fear, almost as though they had become my comfort. In a strange sense it offered stability because it was familiar and, I felt, made up my personality.

Yes, over time I had allowed myself to become those negative emotions. When I realised this, it was like I had opened a door within myself, and from there a new line of communication began. I submitted myself to my heart. I like to think of the heart as the lighthouse of the soul. There is no greater guidance than listening to our heart.

I learnt that without change, there can be no new direction, and although it may be painful at times, it would be necessary for me to face the pain in order to move forward to a new beginning – the one my heart longed for. So I began to quiet my overactive thought process and listen to my heart. This allowed me to be flexible enough to seek change, hungry enough to want change, and focused enough to begin to change!

11. Time to Talk

To accomplish my mission, I was going to have to address my childhood traumas – the abandonment, the sexual abuse, and the attempted murder I survived. I knew that these were the root cause issues I had never dealt with in my time here on Earth. Being truly alone for the first time in years, with only myself to argue with, it became apparent to me that now was the time I needed to talk. After listening to the AA Zoom meeting online, I also realised that I may help others by sharing my story. Something clicked within my mind. If I could somehow help someone else by sharing my recovery and the events of my childhood, then it would be worthwhile.

I had nothing left to lose. I knew that if I was going to do this, I had to go all the way. I knew that there were family members, school friends, and work colleagues on my Facebook page. How could I begin to speak about my past? How could I let them into the darkest areas of my soul? How would it be received? Was I just opening myself up to "humiliation? If I were going to use my video journal as a form of therapy, I had to discuss what was hurting me. Although I had briefly mentioned that I had been abused as a child, I had never gone into detail.

But it was nagging me. Being a man and talking about being raped is no easy process. I am not saying it's any easier for a woman – of course not. I work in an all-male environment where the testosterone levels are through the roof. By sharing my story, I was exposing my vulnerabilities. When I gave this some serious thought, I realised it is because people don't speak about these things that makes them so taboo. I thought back to my gramps when he used to say 'Look me in the eye and shame the devil.' I am not the one who should feel shame. If someone gets robbed, they tell people, and the world reflects back their pain with support and kindness. But when someone has been sexually abused as a child or is suffering from an addiction, it feels to the survivor that their pain is reflected back with a coldness that forces them to withdraw into the shadows, alone and frightened. So the only way we survive is to submerge our story. In doing so, negative behaviour patterns form a coping mechanism to ensure we keep our pain buried deep within, locked away in the abyss as we continue to spiral, and no one understands why.

This was no easy task for me, but in many ways, I feel it was the best thing I could do for my own recovery. I started to write about my past and then speak on camera. This was the first time I had talked about my dark history with a sober mind, and as I typed each word, I felt as though I was giving the little boy who always wanted to fly back his voice. Once I had opened up, the words began to flow, cleansing me of the burdens and baggage I had carried with me for so long. I felt free, and through the many messages I received, I knew that I was not alone. I was right that many people struggled to speak about their childhood traumas. Later in life, they, too, were experiencing battles with alcohol or other drugs.

I was beginning to feel stronger within myself and in regard to my recovery. Empowered by the written and spoken word, I broke the chains that had kept me anchored to the past for so many years. I had never been a believer in

81

counselling or talking therapies. But this has changed now for me. If you can find someone to talk to, to confide in, either a qualified therapist or a dear and close friend, regarding any challenges you are facing or struggles life has thrown your way, I encourage you to reach out.

By talking, we lighten our load and have a means of breaking away from the demons that taunt us from within the cages of our minds and our hearts. I also recommend journaling, either in video or written form. Every word you write is an emotional expression of what you are going through and can be the first step towards seeking the help and support you may need. In many ways, I feel that writing saved my life and pulled me out of the whirlpool of addiction. It served as a means for me to lighten the load of thoughts and pressures that I was dealing with. It was also a means for me to successfully strategise and plan the route that I would embark on to climb the mountain and gain some peace – not just peace of mind but also peace of heart.

The struggle to sleep was difficult; I'd wake up feeling tired and face the day trying to think of different things to keep my mind occupied with a positive focus and outlook. If the days were busy, things were more manageable, but if I didn't have much on, I would wake up stressing about having idle hands. So I started to notice other things I could do. At the flat where I was living, there was a garden and it was in a bit of a shambles. The weather was warm. So I decided to tackle that. I have never been a keen gardener. However, in the early days, being especially busy and productive felt right for me.

The cravings really started to hit me badly at around day three alcohol-free. As I went about my typical day, all I saw was people sitting around with cans in their hands and enjoying the sun. I'd never noticed that many people drinking in parks before as I drove through London. With my state of mind at that time, it seemed everyone was drinking the amber nectar besides me.

The summertime was always a fantastic excuse for a cold beer after work. It is the norm for so many people. Beer garden weather or out in the garden at home having those lazy evenings of relaxation with a well-deserved cold one after a hard day's graft. Everyone's at it, so it stood to reason that I would enjoy this simple pleasure. When these thoughts began to seep into my internal monologue, I had to check in with myself. *Yes, Matt, that's all very well for most people, but you are not most people. You're thinking about that first refreshing sip of alcohol on a hot summer's day. But, Matt, think about how the night goes on. You can never just stop at that one, two, or even three. Hell, you can't even just have a four-pack! You never enjoy just a relaxing drink; this is a sugar-coated image of the actual reality. You always drink to get drunk – simple.*

Our subconscious mind only ever thinks about that quick fix, that first mouthful of alcohol. I often had to remind myself of the truth that whenever I have the slightest sniff of booze, everything changes from what could have been a lovely evening to disaster. I know this. The problem was that my drinking had become an automatic behaviour when out and about with colleagues and friends, triggering me into submission through no fault of their own.

Due to lockdown, people were even sitting in their front gardens having a nice glass of prosecco – fuck me, even when I turn the corner onto my road, there they are. 'Well, we are in lockdown, so what else can we do?' There was no escaping it, and at times I had to grit my teeth and push through the storm.

I was aware and used my video log to express how I felt – mostly when the internal dialogue was becoming overwhelming and my cravings were surfacing. The pulling in my stomach and frustration in my mind, a hunger that was devouring me from the inside out. The more I tried to ignore it, the more significant the pull would become. So I would bring my attention to it.

12. Dealing with Triggers and Cravings

I decided that I had to face things head-on if I was going to crack this and finally succeed. I began to make a list of situations that were a high risk for me regarding relapsing. I identified my triggers as best I could through self-observation. I began to make lists, looking into feelings, thoughts, people, and places.

Feelings

What feelings tended to trigger my desire for alcohol? Here I listed both good and bad things, such as a stressful day at work, having the next day off work, a reason for celebration, or having a low day and feeling anxious or depressed, etc.

Thoughts

I listed the thoughts that would rampage through my mind like a steam train. An internal monologue would say stuff like 'Have a drink, Matt, you deserve it. I'll give up tomorrow. If I don't have a drink, how will I sleep? Everyone expects me to drink, so I might as well. It'll be boring without alcohol.'

People

I thought about the people I encountered who increased my desire for alcohol, like being around colleagues when all they talked about was going to the pub. Sometimes I felt that way after talking on the phone or visiting certain family members. I felt nagged or like people were trying to control my drinking.

Places

Under places, I also thought about events and special days such as Christmas and birthdays, watching a movie, going out for a meal, or having a family barbecue.

By writing my list, I was becoming productive. I also made myself aware of the many situations and circumstances that trigger my desire for a drink – and there are many. This was the first encouraging step I began to take for my recovery. List in hand, I began to focus on how I could combat those situations. I knew that the list would be pointless if a trigger occurred and I was unaware of allowing myself to go into autopilot mode, so I decided to bring my attention to my cravings when this happened.

Back in 2011, I had become very interested in Buddhist teachings. I actually completed a course in mindfulness life coaching alongside several other mindfulness and meditation courses. Unfortunately, I never did anything worthwhile with this knowledge. I wasn't yet ready to deal with my own problems, childhood traumas, and addictions.

When I began this recovery journey in May 2020, I researched my problem. I tried to find a means to combat my addictions, helping me move towards an alcohol-free life that would be fulfilled and happy.

While I was beavering away on my PC, I came across several articles on mindfulness, which made me think back to the information I had learnt years ago. I still had all my old notes and essays on my computer and started clicking on them, opening up the files like I was opening up a treasure chest. I felt like Indiana Jones stumbling across something special that had been hidden in the desert for hundreds of years. But this information had not been buried in some far-off sandy dune. Instead, it was locked away within the cobweb-filled, darkest areas of my own mind.

Mindfulness is the practice of becoming consciously aware of our feelings, thoughts, and sensations within the body using meditation practice. Please do not panic, my friend; this book is not taking a turn into some deep and spiritual pathway, and I am not evolving into a guru of any kind. But I would like to take a moment to share some handy tools that I remembered from what I learnt about mindfulness all those years ago.

I found in my own recovery that by becoming aware of what's going on in both my inner and my outer world, I can give myself back choice instead of merely running on autopilot.

When I talk about autopilot, I am talking about the internal monologue that we continuously play on a loop within our minds. We all tend to go through life blissfully unaware of the autopilot mindset. It forces us to respond to situations and circumstances based on previous encounters and events or on what we have learned from others, including our parents' opinions and teachings.

Rather than seeing situations and circumstances as separate, standalone moments in our life, the autopilot takes command. We simply react based on past experience. I believe this keeps us going round and round on the habit carousel.

Let's look at how the autopilot is related to our cravings and triggers. A craving can arise in various forms: as a feeling or sensation, as words within your thought process, or as an image seen in your mind's eye.

By learning to be more aware of our thoughts and feelings, we can spot the craving as it begins to form. Usually, when an urge arises, we get a physical sensation quickly followed by words, such as 'I need a drink,' or imagery as quick as a flash of said drink. We then tend to go on autopilot and simply believe the statement 'I need a drink' as the solution to ease the craving.

Because we now have the mindset that this is what we need to have, we continue to pursue the drink to satisfy the craving. The craving becomes stronger until we have what we think we need to ease the urge based on our previous encounters. This is our subconscious mind at work.

Instead of having an automatic response to the craving, by being present and aware, you can now choose instead of being ruled by the automatic response created by the subconscious mind. We can get back choice by bringing our attention very gently to the sensation or thought that fuels the craving. We can witness what is going on within ourselves without acting on the impulse. To do this, it helps if you begin training your mind. Think of your mind as a muscle like any other; it needs exercise to strengthen and develop. I had to become a personal trainer for my mind to maintain an awareness, spot my triggers and cravings, and then make the best choice for me.

To do this, I thought it was important to bring moments of self-awareness into my day-to-day life. Times when I would stop briefly and check in with myself to calm the thought process of the autopilot for just a few seconds, allowing me to feel my bodily sensations and witness my mental state. I wanted to have moments of mindful pause at random times, similar to how a trigger or craving can show its ugly head at unexpected moments. This would get me used to stopping the autopilot and becoming aware. I wanted to practise bringing myself into the present moment, the here and now, where I knew I could regain power over the autopilot. I thought that the more I did this, the easier it would become to spot triggers and cravings and combat them.

But how would I do it? I needed little reminders throughout my day, and I came up with a few ideas, but they didn't seem practical. I could use post-it notes, but then I figured *do I really want post-it notes all over the house? And what about when I'm out and about, like at work? I can't keep post-it notes stuck to my forehead or all over my lorry cab.* Then I thought maybe I could set an alarm on my phone. No, that wouldn't work because I wouldn't have the randomness that I felt I needed. Although some triggers can be at certain times of day, my cravings were often triggered at the most random times when I least expected them.

I needed a different way to remind myself. I was going to have to give this some thought. As I pondered my decision to bring moments of mindful pause into every day, I sat staring out of my kitchen window. A huge crow came and landed on my fence outside. This black beauty caught my eye, as I have always loved crows. The folklore surrounding them and the mystery of this magnificent master of the skies here in urban England had always intrigued me, and I felt an affinity with them. I love crows. When I drive in my truck, it can seem like a lonely experience. But if I look out of my window, I can often see a crow atop a lamp post, treetop, or aerial, like a guardian watching over my journey and keeping me company on those long winding roads.

Lightbulb moment, Matt! Perfect! I thought I would set an intention. When I see a crow, I will stop for a moment if it's safe to do so, focus on the crow, then bring my attention to my breath while calming my thought process.

During this pause, I check in with myself. How am I feeling? I allow my internal dialogue to quieten by bringing my attention fully to this present moment in time. I do this just for a few seconds. As the days went on, I tried to extend these mindful pauses, exercising my mindset of bringing moments of calm and taking over the reins from the autopilot.

Perfect! The crow would become not only my guardian on the road but now an assistant in my recovery. The wonderful thing about choosing something found in nature as your reminder is that when you bring yourself altogether into the present, no one needs to be aware of what you are doing. You do not need to stop, get into the lotus position, start chanting mantras, or roll out a mat and begin performing yoga on impulse.

These moments are known as active meditation and can be done anywhere, just like that. As you pause and check in with yourself, if any thoughts come from the autopilot's hideous script that are pulling your attention towards an event of the past or something in the future, gently let it go. Bring your attention back to your breath and this present moment. That is how I started to exercise my mind and utilise the most effective tool I had at my disposal when dealing with triggers and cravings.

The simple mindfulness technique of S.T.O.P.

This is a very simple acronym that we can use when we react to situations and circumstances on autopilot. When I think about my own addictions, I often view myself as acting beyond my own control, on autopilot, so I figured that if I could be consistent in remembering to use this mindfulness technique, it may help me change my typical behaviour pattern.

This is how it goes

When I observe a trigger or craving emerging within myself, I don't try to dismiss it. Instead, I bring my attention to it.

Stop

I stop myself in my tracks as soon as I feel a craving.

Take a breath

This momentary pause allows me to go from the autopilot in my mind to the here and now, giving me back control.

Observe myself

During this pause, I look at the craving and think of what my body actually needs and not what my mind thinks it wants – that is, alcohol. I often notice that I haven't eaten. *Okay, Matt, get some grub. That will take the edge off.* I'm stressed – *okay, Matt, get some fresh air.* I'm bored and lacking stimuli – *okay, Matt, do something productive. This feeling will pass!*

Proceed

I then proceed with what is needed, and I often had to grit my teeth and be disciplined, but I did get through it. I use this simple technique as and when needed to help me regain control, giving me back choice. This allows me to respond rather than react to triggers and cravings. With my list, I was able to be prepared for my trigger times, and I was committed to making my recovery the most important thing in my life. I planned and prepared for my trigger times by getting productive.

My confidence and focus became more determined, as I now had a tool at my disposal, but this was no time for me to sit back and rest on my laurels. No way. I knew that

S.T.O.P. was not going to be enough, so I started to ask myself what I did of an evening when I was drinking. The answer was nothing. I just sat alone most nights, necking drink after drink while watching some crap on Netflix.

This was boredom.

I knew that a lack of stimuli in the evening would put me in the danger zone, so I decided to learn about my problem. I signed up for online courses, as I felt that the more I knew about alcoholism, the greater the advantage I could gain over my demons. It was time for me to get busy. I started to plan and prepare my recovery properly.

13. Attacking My Problem

As a child, I would spend hours planning and arranging my toy soldiers into formations, strategising and finding the best means of taking cover and the perfect points for my armies to begin their attack. I came to look at my recovery in the same way, and I called it 'attacking my problem'. I didn't want to sit back and wait for my triggers and cravings to take hold, and I felt within my heart that this time around, I needed to get proactive. But I do recommend that anyone going into recovery first contacts their GP, finds their local support groups, and takes advantage of all the help out there.

I was in the first lockdown. Visits to the doctor were being discouraged, and support groups were closed due to the dreaded covid-19. I also work in a job where I never know what time I will be home in the evening, so committing to anything will always be a problem. This was one of my many excuses in the past, one of the reasons why I could not break away from my addictions. But not this time. This time, I was going to get strategic, plan, and prepare. I intended to take my recovery by the horns, and in doing so, I was determined to take back control over my life. The one thing the army has taught me is that discipline bridges the gap between goals and accomplishments. I knew I had to be disciplined in my approach.

I grabbed my trusty pen and began to think about what it is in life I want or need. What is it that will make my life feel accomplished or rewarding? I started to write things down and circle them. I came up with the usual wants, hopes, and desires that we all have, such as more money, a better career, nice holidays, more family time, a bigger house, etc. – the list went on. I sat there for a while, pondering what I had written, thinking *that cannot be it. There must be something more.* Then I had a lightbulb moment. What could I do to accomplish all these material things, and even then, what could I do to truly level up my life? Then it hit me. Break the cycle.

My nan used to say she felt our family was cursed. We never seemed to have any luck and always seemed to struggle in life. When God did give us a golden carrot, he seemed to have a giant rabbit hop in and take it from us. This had appeared to be a continuous cycle throughout the generations. I wanted my life to be different; more importantly, I wanted better for my kids. *Matt, you have to break the cycle.*

For me to start to do this, I needed to begin setting goals, and as I did, I acknowledged that the primary goal, the big dream, was not actually to get sober. The main goal was to live the life I was born to live and not the one that had been moulded by my past. Becoming sober was one part of that, one stepping stone to accomplishing my ultimate goal. I needed to get strategic and face my recovery head-on. The first thing I knew I would have to do was combat my triggers and cravings, as I spoke about previously. These were the parts of myself that I would be facing on the battlefield each day in skirmishes that would decide whether I lapsed or came out of each day the victor.

I also looked into a thing known as a habit loop. A habit loop consists of a trigger, a routine, and a reward. The trigger is the thing that sets the loop in motion, the routine is the action that we take, and the reward is the outcome of the habit loop. For me, the habit was drinking daily to the point of blackout or at the very least so that I could knock myself out at bedtime. I had many triggers that enabled this.

However, the main one I was conscious of was that once my working day was done, I settled in, waiting for the night and the dream time to begin. My trigger was the evening, my habit was drinking, and my reward was passing out until morning. I feared bedtime so much that the prospect of going to bed without alcohol in my system filled me with anxiety. It was hard for me to think of anything else as the night drew in.

I was aware of this, so I decided to bring in new habits and change my behaviour pattern. I wanted to change from sitting alone getting wasted every night to positive behaviours that offered rewarding stimuli and kept me busy until bedtime. I figured that I worked long hours; by keeping busy of an evening, I should be able to sleep. Other people managed it, so I should too.

I focused first on my routine. To bring in a new habit loop, I needed to change my behaviour to be more productive and fulfilling. I spent a great deal of time looking at various hobbies and interests and thinking about my timings regarding mealtimes and showering. I also thought about how much time I just sat staring at the TV. This was no good for me. The TV offered no decent stimuli to keep me focused or motivated, so it had to go.

I found that I enjoyed writing, and I wanted to learn as much as I could about my problem. I studied many books and completed some online substance and alcohol abuse courses. After work, I would get home, stick my dinner on, fire up the computer, and then jump in the shower. Then I would eat my dinner, easing any initial cravings, before settling down to either write or study. I did the same routine every day, and although I had moments when cravings would begin to appear, I was able to cope with them by allowing them to flow over me like a wave. Knowing what was happening and that the sensation would pass, I responded with positive, productive behaviour.

This was not easy, I admit, and I really did have to grit my teeth and ride the wave out. I found that once I got to around nine or ten o'clock, I was okay again. I changed my routine with consistency, and some nights I had to force myself to stick to that routine. After around three months, a new habit loop had begun to form. Instead of thinking about alcohol during the day, I was excited to write an article or complete a module of my course. The cravings were not as impactful as they had once been.

By taking one day at a time and not focusing on the next day, week, month, or even year, I found I was getting on top of things, but I knew I had to remain consistent and not let my guard down. Consistency and discipline had become my best friends during that time.

14. Let's Talk about Attaining Goals!

Earlier in the book, I briefly touched on the need to set goals. Goal setting is vitally important for us to remain focused, which helps us to have consistency in our recovery process. Goal setting is equally important in many other areas of our lives. We all have different aims in life. You may be thinking *I want to change* but struggle to accomplish your goals, and perhaps you never felt you could attain your hopes and dreams?

I struggled with this all my life. Relapse after relapse after relapse.

I'm never going to drink again.

Relapse.

I'm all about keeping fit now, my new addiction, never drinking again.

Relapse.

I'm going to save all the money I used to spend on drink and go on holiday or get a new car because I'm never going to drink again!

Relapse.

On my current recovery journey, I have found that the more ambitious the goal is, the more drastic and difficult the change has to be in order for me to accomplish said goal. The problem I was having was that I set too high a goal. (I WILL NEVER DRINK AGAIN! Often followed by a fanfare in my mind.)

Way to drastic a change for me to cope. The mountain becomes too steep, I trip, I fall, and my goal falls with me. Back at the bottom, alone, dishevelled, in need of a boost, I turn once more to alcohol, keeping myself in the constant cycle of beginning the climb with all the intentions in the world but doing so very poorly equipped. I was just setting myself up for the fall again and again. So what did I learn this time around?

Simply make the mountain smaller; trade the mountain for stepping stones. This thought popped into my mind while watching *Superman*, of all things, in the scene where he is crying in the closet at school and his mum is trying to coax him out. The young Clark Kent struggles to cope with the noise and other effects of being superhuman in our earthly realm. When he tells his mum the worlds too big, she tells him to make it smaller. This encourages him to tune his focus. I don't know why I thought of this when I was thinking about goals, but I did, and that's what I realised would help me. I needed to make my goals smaller.

When I think of my goals as stepping stones and not a high mountainous climb, I can view things differently. The goal is now across a river and not atop a mountain. This is now what I do. I set small, more easily attainable goals. Each one I view as bringing me closer towards the larger goal of getting across the river.

But I don't focus on the larger goal. I don't want to lose my footing as I step across each stepping stone. I plan the smaller, more manageable goals first. I focus on each one at a time, one day at a time. As I accomplish one, a sense of achievement is granted to me, and this gives me greater confidence in stepping forward to the next stone.

By focusing on the smaller goals, the achievable goals, like just getting through today alcohol-free, I get closer to attaining the larger goal, which in the beginning seemed impossible but over time will become achievable.

Lists are a great tool. I make many of them now, and as I get things sorted, I enjoy ticking them off, working my way across the river to bring about the change I desire.

Ask yourself this: what do you want? How do you desire your life to be? That's your big goal. It's across the river. Grab a pen and paper and start listing the first things you need to do.

For example, you want a better job (big goal).

Stepping Stones

1. Look into the job role you think would best suit you.

2. Find out what skills and qualifications you need for the job.

3. If you haven't got them, find out how you get them and go for it. Then a new list begins, and a new river.

4. Already got the skills? Sort your CV.

5. Get it to potential employers and don't give up!

6. Brush up on interview techniques.

7. Go to the interview.

8. Get the job.

9. Didn't get the job? Observe what you did, make the changes needed, don't give up, and go to the next interview.

10. You messed up a couple of times, but your interview techniques improve. Now you have more experience in interviews because you didn't give up … you're hired, BOOM! Mission accomplished!

Stepping stones can also be used in recovery. I view every day as a stepping stone. I have a larger goal: to live alcohol-free for the rest of my life. This also forms part of the ultimate goal to live the life I desire. But I don't dwell on that larger goal. That's not the goal I set each day. Obviously, it's there, but it's not my focus. I set small goals that I want to attain along the way that offer me a sense of achievement as I move forward. These are my focus, like writing an article by a specific date, which I couldn't do if I were drunk.

My list would be:

1. Eat my meals.

2. Stay aware of how I feel.

3. Be mindful of my triggers.

4. Stay hydrated.

5. Don't get overtired.

6. Motivate myself to sit each evening during my trigger times and write.

7. Article done, and I'm sober, and that is fantastic!

Once I've accomplished that goal, I've done something productive and positive. This increases my confidence as I move into the following day. Before I know it, I'm bringing in good behaviour patterns and moving forward towards an alcohol-free life without that even being my central focus. I guess what I'm saying is look after the small goals, and eventually the larger ones will take care of themselves.

How to Set a Solid Intention

Setting an intention for what you wish to accomplish is often overlooked. Still, this simple practice can help us complete our tasks with drive, focus, and strength.

It is vital that before you begin your task, you spend some time focused on what you are trying to accomplish.

Ask yourself:

What is it I wish to cultivate from this task? What do I hope to accomplish? What do I want to embody during the work that needs to be done? You can think of any question in line with your current mission, whether you are attending a job interview, preparing for home DIY, going for a run, or even cooking dinner. Maybe your intention is to get through today alcohol-free.

When you are ready, set your intention and focus on what is most needed. Once you have your intention set, you don't want to go and forget about it.

Try to be mindful and maintain awareness, carrying the intention with you and remembering to check in with yourself for consistency so that you don't forget. When the day is done, look back and think about the intention you set. How often did you follow it? A journal may come in handy here. Just like when we discussed triggers and cravings, you could set a reminder to bring the intention back into focus.

Try to recall certain moments when your intention came to the fore and give yourself a pat on the back for being aware that you embodied your intention.

You can also set an intention before bedtime to become aware of when you wake up. This could be more of a general intention along the lines of: today I will practice active listening, self-compassion, and gratitude.

The possibilities are fantastic and will help you develop and strengthen a great mindset. I often do this to build empathy, gratitude, and self-compassion, among other things, to assist my own personal growth and to keep myself in check.

Do not confuse intentions with goals! Goals occur in the future, and our intentions are within the present moment. To act according to our intentions can take time and an awful lot of practice. So as you begin, please do not stress or be hard on yourself.

You will, at some point, forget your intention, probably not long after setting it. It's okay even if you only manage to remember it once during your day. That is a fantastic effort!

15. Other People

Sometimes people speak, and they mean well, but they do not know the damage they can do. I felt as though I needed to be open about my drinking problem. I had reached a point where I wanted to talk about it with those closest to me and be honest about my troubles and my addictions. However, when I did, I found that at times, other people's thoughts and opinions became another obstacle that could easily have put me back into the whirlpool of addiction if I had listened to them.

It was important for me to share my issues regarding alcoholism, and in my naivety, I thought people would be understanding and, in turn, help me avoid my triggers. But what I discovered was quite the opposite. It was almost like they were in denial and not me.

As I began to share my feelings and try to talk about how my life was panning out, the response I all too often received was 'You're not an alcoholic, you just like a drink. Everyone's entitled to have a beer, Matt.' I would try to explain that alcohol had become a massive problem in my life and I wanted to pack it in. But still, people didn't listen. One classic comment was: 'You're just giving up for a little while, aren't you? I mean it's not like you're never going to drink again?' Then we would be out, and people would try to encourage me to drink. I struggled with this in my mind for quite some time. I couldn't understand why they would do this.

Let me give you an example. If I came out as a heroin addict, I'm pretty sure people wouldn't be encouraging me to indulge in some skag or say to me, 'What, so you're never going to jack up again?' They just wouldn't – well, aside from my dealer. Of course, he would be distraught.

When it comes to alcohol, people often take a different stance. Many people still perceive an alcoholic as a stereotypical old wino drinking out of a brown paper bag in the park or having vodka on their cornflakes. Sadly, this isn't the case, and there are far more people in this world, in our civilised modern society, struggling with alcoholism than we realise. This is because alcohol is so widely accepted. Most of these individuals are high-functioning, respectable people who carry out their jobs successfully and live normal lives by day.

But I bet you any money that if you were to ask their partners or spouses if they felt these people had a drinking problem, the response you would get would shock many. I'll use myself as an example. I was very good at wearing a mask, and people would only see the Matt that I wanted them to see. They would never guess that behind closed doors of an evening, I would sit alone, the alcohol would flow, and my persona would change to someone who was uncaring, aggressive, irresponsible, and depressive. This was due to drinking. I used alcohol as a means to cope with the day-to-day struggles of life, as a means to relieve boredom, and as a means to forget the traumas of my past.

To continue on this journey of recovery, in many ways, I had to learn to have a thicker skin towards people around me, although my mindset and perspective did become more flexible over time. I found I was becoming more empathic towards others. I did, however, have to become steadfast and focused on what I knew within my heart was the direction that I needed to go In. If we cannot stay aware of this, we play a risky game by taking on board the opinions of others who do not know the whole truth.

There is a very good chance that if you are embarking on a journey of sobriety, like me, you have become a master manipulator and liar over time. You would have been able to hoodwink an awful lot of people into believing that you live as a normal, respectable person who likes a few cans at night just like everyone else. So it stands to reason that many will think you are overreacting or going through a phase when you tell people you have a drinking problem.

Kind of like my short-lived vegan phase; many people just humoured me, thinking it wouldn't be long until I was drooling over a Big Mac. Yes, they were right, sadly. You will get those people, and there will be others, of course, the ones who are very similar to you, and when you say you want to pack up drinking or that you are an alcoholic, you are holding up a mirror to them, and they don't like what they see because they're in denial about their own alcohol intake or lifestyle choices.

They will want to keep you drinking to make themselves feel better, but you have to do what is best for your life and your future. The problem is that many of these well-wishers may be family members who do not want to accept that you are an alcoholic, and a lot of this can come down to the stigma attached to the label of alcoholism. It is challenging for anyone opening up regarding an addiction such as alcoholism.

If someone opens up to you, listen to them and try to empathise with them as best as you can, to see their point of view. I know it's very difficult to understand addiction if you have not been enslaved to one. Let's take smoking, for instance. Non-smokers cannot understand why smokers find it so hard to quit or even what enjoyment they gain from a cigarette in the first place.

This is the same for people who are not alcoholics. If you do not have a drinking problem but are reading this book to gain insight regarding someone you know, or to know the mind of an addict better, it will help if you can try to see things from the addict's perspective. Acknowledge how they feel as you attempt to understand and then support them in their decision to change and seek help. The person suffering from alcoholism is doing something courageous by reaching for support and opening up. This should be commended and not brushed over or ignored.

While we are on the subject of other people and their perspectives, let's touch on something quickly. I never considered what triggered my drinking and negative behaviour patterns before this journey. Naturally, I had to learn to understand why people were focusing on my reaction to triggers, which was the strong desire to get off my face instead of figuring out why I felt I had to – that is, get to the root cause.

It's natural for people to concentrate their attention on the trigger's aftermath and not on the trigger itself. I understand this because all too often, we only see what's directly in front of our eyes. If it doesn't fit in with normal, socially acceptable behaviour, you are immediately judged and condemned. Just as people do not see behind closed doors, it can be difficult for them to comprehend the extent of our drinking. When they see the aftermath of my overindulgence, the focus becomes that and not what triggered it.

Although I didn't portray it to the world, within myself, I felt like I was a waste of space (a term I had used when judging others). My triggers never came up in conversation because I didn't know or understand what they were. So why would other people? I couldn't expect them to, and once again, we discuss the need to view things from different perspectives.

It most certainly is a big ask to expect someone to focus on the trigger rather than the behaviour, because they are often suffering deeply from the addiction along with the addict. However, I would like to point out that although many view beauty as skin deep, addiction is not. There is a lot more complexity to the pathways that lead to a habit, which, for many, cause pain, suffering, guilt, and anguish.

I have spent the last year unravelling mine, and the more I untangled, the more I realised that by taking the time to understand what led someone to addiction, we can, in many cases, discover the root causes. Then healing can begin and new pathways unfold. By triggers, I mean what triggered my gateway into addiction alongside what situations or circumstances fired up my cravings.

I struggled to sleep, so drinking in the evening became a regular behaviour pattern to the point where I felt I would not get through the night without alcohol, which caused me great distress.

When I was sexually assaulted as a child, my abuser gave me alcohol, solvents, and drugs. These helped me become numb, pass out, lose inhibitions, and forget. Later in life, alcohol and drugs became my form of self-medication when I was going through stress or pain or when I needed confidence or was struggling to cope with life. It was my go-to method of healing as a youngster, and it carried easily over to my adult years as a natural behaviour pattern because it was all I knew to help me cope.

This is why I believe it is vital we take the time to understand the triggers behind the behaviour without casting judgement.

The Judgements of Others

One of the most challenging barriers to recovery and when struggling with childhood trauma is fearing others' judgements when we first begin to open up and seek support. Sadly, this is such a significant issue that it all too often stops people from seeking the help they so badly need. The cycle of addiction continues with depression, guilt, and shame, to name but a few.

I've encountered judgements from others my whole life. Every time I begin to open up about my past, I can feel the atmosphere change as whoever I am with starts to feel uneasy. I guess I understand this because of the taboo nature of what I'm preparing to talk about. I decided that I needed to begin to open up in order to fully recover from my addictions. If this makes people feel uncomfortable, that's their problem and not mine.

My recovery and wellbeing far outweigh the ignorant opinions of others. Here are a few handy tips I came up with to help myself deal with those judgements, ensuring I could hold my head high and progress as I needed to. First and foremost, ignore them and don't take anything personally. This can be very difficult, I know. Still, it is essential to remember that others' views and opinions are often a reflection of the person's own reality and how they view things. This does not make their argument the truth.

When I get judged regarding my past, I do not allow it to bother me anymore. I shrug my shoulders and think *how could they understand if they have never been in my situation?* Be compassionate to these judgmental folks.

But why would you show them compassion, Matt? Judgmental and nasty people are not born that way. They are made that way. When I encounter people like this, I try to think about what happened to this person to make them end up this way. What judgements did they experience growing up? What did they learn from their parents? Although it doesn't excuse their behaviour, I have actually learnt to show empathy towards people who seek to judge me for my past and my recovery.

Don't become defensive. When we become overly defensive, we quickly begin to shrink to their level. When that happens, we actually feed them the power to continue. Often, they want the reaction, the debate, or the argument. Don't give it to them. You will come away angry and bitter, ruining your day because of their ignorance … Don't let it!

See those with judging eyes for who they really are. By this, I mean that when people cast judgements, they often have similar issues in their own lives. They just haven't faced up to them yet. I have experienced many trolls since starting my video log online. One of the strange things, which I did not expect, is that a few messaged me privately to apologise, stating that they had been through similar life experiences as me. I guess their lashing out at me was a cry for help in many ways, like the old saying: people in glass houses shouldn't throw stones. When I was caught up in my own addictions, I was guilty of looking at others and labelling them as an alcoholic or a junkie.

When I did this, my words were really just a reflection of how I saw myself, and this is the case of many who judge us, sadly. Focus your attention on those who love and support you, and most certainly do not believe or listen to the judgements!

Avoid those who set out to judge you. You do not need their opinions bringing you down. Gradually they will turn their attention to someone else. Very importantly, please do not believe in their judgements. They are not fact!

If someone calls you worthless, it does not mean you are. You are worth a great deal to this world and those who live in it. Never get pulled into their negativity! Many people who freely cast judgements on others enjoy tearing people down and often take great pride in it. This is a shallow attempt to make themselves feel better. What does that tell you about them? Never let others drag you down. Sadly, this is a lesson I have learnt throughout Year One, but I did choose to go through my recovery on a very public forum. I put myself out there and have encountered many attacks from trolls both online and in the flesh. I have learnt on this journey, however, that the shame is not on me. The guilt resides with the predator who stole my innocence and the monster that led me to the gateway of my addictions, opened the doors, and threw me in.

16. I Was Stronger Than I Thought

The first seventy-six days of my recovery brought me many challenges. Still, I never expected to have to experience losing three family members. First, my nan – without her, this journey probably would never have begun. Then on Day 49 alcohol-free, as I was planning what I was going to do for Day 50, I had a phone call to tell me my father had died, and then again, on Day 76, my uncle passed away.

They say things come in threes, and this devastating time sent my head into a complete spin, not only for my own pain but also for the pain I knew my son Tyler was going to feel, particularly as we were right in the middle of a lockdown. He had gone through so much already, not least that a few weeks before, I had moved out of the family home. His world had been turned upside down. Although my dad wasn't great with me growing up, he was close to Tyler, and I felt that in many ways he had tried to make up for his mistakes as a father by being a better granddad.

Three deaths, two very unexpected, and here I was trying to stay sober. The evening my dad died was my Day 49. I had been sober for nearly fifty days, and this was a challenge I never expected to come up against. I suppose this is the difficulty with going into recovery. We can be caught off guard, unprepared and vulnerable. After I had heard the news, I sat in my garden, I answered a few calls, and then I decided to go to the shop.

At this point in my mind, I was relapsing. I was prepared to throw my sobriety away and allow myself to slip back into old habits as a means to make myself feel better. This was my first instinct. Even after forty-nine days sober, my autopilot stepped in. It began to take the lead, ushering me into my car and heading towards the shop.

While I was en route, I decided to make a video for my Facebook page. You can see it there on Day 49 alcohol-free. I felt I should make the video explaining what had happened. I had always been honest with the camera. I tried to show my recovery, sweaty bedsheets, agitated moods and everything. I felt that to remain authentic, I needed to pull over and explain what had happened.

In the video, I explained that I was going to the shop to buy some tea. The liar was returning, as I knew in my heart that my intention was not to buy tea. I told myself, 'Matt, have a drink; no one will blame you. No one will even know. You have had devastating news. You'll get back on the wagon, but tonight you can take a step back from the sober path and allow yourself alcohol to make you feel better. You know you'll end up drinking, don't kid yourself.'

I argued with myself mentally, but the pull to buy alcohol was so strong. In my head, I held that same fixation that had always gripped me once the cravings took hold and gained the upper hand. Day 49 alcohol-free nearly became the night I caved in. Instead, it became the night I overcame my addictions in the face of great adversity. I was feeling pain, anger, loss, and grief, to name just a few of the many emotions taking over. Day 49 alcohol-free became the night I proved to myself that I could cope and not give up. Everything came down to one defining moment, and I would like to share that with you now. You can check out my video on Day 53 alcohol-free, explaining what went through my mind that evening and the events that occurred.

So I found myself being pulled back into the want for alcohol. Without thinking about Sharon's feelings or Tyler's, I was only concerned about myself. Selfish, alcoholic Matt was back in the room, and I know many people would say, 'It's okay, your dad has just died. It's understandable.' I know even Sharon would have let me off the hook for that one. I made my video and was on a fast course towards our local shop with one thing on my mind. I have to tell you this because if I'm not honest, then there's no point in what I'm trying to put across.

I entered the shop while a battle was going on within myself. I had more excuses to drink rampaging through my mind than I had reasons not to drink. My biggest excuse was that people would understand, and anyone would need a drink after hearing such devastating news. I was telling myself *people will be expecting me to drink. Sharon will expect me to drink. They will expect it. It's what you do, and they will understand.* This was the internal monologue that played on loop as I was walking up the aisles towards the alcohol section.

En route, I grabbed a box of tea, but this was the deceiver coming out. The cunning, manipulative alcoholic was back in the game. *If I walk in with tea but I also have alcohol, I can go down the lines of saying I had a good intention. I bought the tea, but I had to get the booze. My dad's just died; I need it.* I knew no one would have a go at me. I basically had a free pass. These were the moments I looked for as an alcoholic – those nights when I felt my drinking would be accepted due to circumstances beyond my control. The nights that warranted the need for alcohol according to how our society typically responds to situations.

I was in the queue, which was longer than usual due to lockdown and social distancing. As I said earlier, shops always seem to direct their queue down the alcohol aisle. When you are an alcoholic, this is like being a lion at the watering hole. So much choice; what to devour first?

I looked at the lager as I waited in the queue but thought *no, tonight's not a lager night*. My eyes turned to behind the counter. I used to be rather partial to dark rum. My gaze became a steady focus on the rum. I was losing the battle and the autopilot was taking over. The queue steadily went down, and in front of me was a group of kids getting their shopping. It looked as though their mum had sent them to the shops. They also had a selection of sweets, which was probably their payment for going.

They seemed to be taking a while, and I started to get agitated. *Come on, kids, I mean, after all, my dad has just died and I need rum.* I wondered why they were taking so long, and I pulled my attention away from the glistening bottle of rum towards them while letting out a disgruntled huff. I noticed their card bounced; their mum must have given them her card, but it didn't have enough funds for the kids to make their purchase. They tried a couple of times, got on the phone with their mum, tried again, and the queue was mounting up behind me. The guy behind the counter could probably see I was becoming agitated. He asked the kids to leave their shopping there and get the funds from their mum or call her from outside the shop.

The kids seemed upset, embarrassed, and confused. They had their sweets all ready to go, and then the bank card said *no, sorry, not today*. You know how kids are; getting a few sweets is a big deal to them. One little boy was no older than Tyler, and to be honest, I don't think they had a great deal.

They stepped aside and it was my turn to go to the till. The shopkeeper lifted the kids' shopping to one side. I looked at the little boy next to me, who had tears in his eyes. I looked back to the shopkeeper, and as he said 'Sorry about that; what can I get you, sir?' I had a moment. In that split second, I breathed, and I became fully present. I was in that room, and I wasn't in my head. I looked at those kids' shopping. I looked at their faces. I was in the room, and I thought about the bottle of rum – say £15 or whatever it was – and I said to the guy, 'Put the kids' stuff back through the till. I'll pay for it.' He looked at me, bemused, and said 'What?' I replied, 'The kids' shopping. Put it back through the till. I'll pay for it, and I will have this box of tea, please.'

I paid for it, picked up my box of tea, and walked out of the shop past the kids. I looked at one and just said 'I got your shopping' and walked out. I had to get out of there. The little boy ran out after me and shouted 'Thank you.' I waved my hand and said 'No worries.' I got in my car and cried my eyes out. I cried and I cried and I cried, thinking *Matt, you were this close to throwing everything away*.

Something happened in that shop that brought me back, away from the chaos of my mind into the present moment. At that moment, I thought *I can buy a bottle of rum or I can put a smile on these kids' faces*. I realised I have a son and a daughter, and I want to keep smiles on their faces. My dad died, and he was an alcoholic. I will be damn sure I'm not putting my kids through the same pain I am feeling right now.

I cried in the car, went home, but felt good. I made my cup of tea; I took a photo of the tea and I put it up on the page. But there was a gnat's cock in it; I nearly caved. Being able to bring myself into the present gave me back choice and made me aware of what was the right thing to do for myself and others. Yes, I was upset that my father had just passed away. Still, that night I proved to myself that I was stronger than I thought. It demonstrated to me that we only need a few seconds to bring ourselves present enough to succeed.

The importance of our conscious decisions and making a decision on impulse should never be overlooked. I firmly believe that this was a decisive moment in my recovery that could have gone either way.

After that day, I found coping with challenges easier; my confidence in myself was more substantial. I knew I had the tools to overcome. I just had to keep going with consistency, motivation, determination, and awareness.

17. Christmas 2020

Another challenge was fast approaching, prepared to storm my recovery like an army of White Walkers storming the wall in *Game of Thrones*. I felt anxious about the upcoming festivities that, year after year, I had ruined in one way or another through my drinking and selfishness.

Christmas should be a time for family and children. It is a time for magical experiences and for everyone to feel loved and appreciated. Sadly, over the years, on many occasions, I had stolen the attention from the day by slipping into my old routine like a soft pair of slippers and waking up on Boxing Day with a path of devastation behind me.

Oh yeah, I was well aware of this now with my sober mind. I had three weeks off work. That is a lot of time to be sitting around idle, surrounded by alcohol-filled shops and discussions everywhere on a party theme. Even though we were in a lockdown, people would still be celebrating at home, still planning to get smashed, and I was set to be out of the loop.

Many anxieties kept the busy autopilot of my mind happy with chaos. How would I have fun? *How will I be the fun, Dad? Once Christmas is over, I am still off work; what am I going to do with myself if I can't drink?*

You will notice the anxieties were still very self-centred – me, me, me, complaints and excuses. I was very much in danger of the old Matt making an appearance. I had to decide and set the intention that this year would be all about my son and Sharon. I am a fortunate man in many respects, and I needed to remind myself of that. Sharon is so supportive of me that Christmas was not going to be the best for her either, as in many ways, when I went into recovery, so did she. She had to deal with my moods and emotional roller coasters, and being the kind woman that she is, she also stopped drinking, so Christmas for her was going to be wine-free.

I did tell her that I didn't mind if she drank, but she said no, she wanted an alcohol-free Christmas, so that's what we did.

Waking up on Christmas morning was certainly different. I was actually up before Tyler and had to wake him up! Wow, that one shocked me, as I expected him to be jumping on our bed in the early hours, but no, I was up first. We got up, went downstairs, and it was terrific. There was no hangover, no tiredness from the Baileys on Christmas Eve, but instead I was entirely focused on my family – and what a day it was. We played Just Dance on the PS4, karaoke, board games, charades, and there was laughter all day.

But the best moment was when Tyler went to bed that night and told us it was the best Christmas ever. I feel quite emotional when I think about it now. We had all been through a lot that year with the lockdown, me leaving, my nan dying, then my dad and my uncle. But we had survived, and as a family. I moved back to our home. I now feel we are stronger than ever. Although it was difficult, with some huge challenges, I know that recovery was the best thing I could have done for myself and our little family unit.

I wasn't entirely out of the woods yet, though. I still had a while before I was due back at work. I was still in the danger zone. When off work, how would I keep myself busy? Sharon went back to work before I did. Tyler was playing online with his mates a lot of the time, and with the lockdown, there wasn't much to do.

Many years ago, I used to enjoy decoupage, which is a means of upcycling furniture by sticking pictures onto it with glue, then varnishing it. Tyler had an old chest of drawers that didn't seem to fit a young lad's room. For a long time, I had been promising to fix his room up, but as we all know, I always put alcohol first, so it never happened.

Sharon said to me, 'Why don't you have a go at decoupaging Tyler's chest of drawers? That will certainly keep you busy.' I thought about this and decided it was a great idea. Completing a craft or similar activity takes focus and motivation. This would be ideal for me, and if I could manage to finish it, seeing his face at the end would be so rewarding. I have been a comic book collector for many years. I know that the artwork and paper density is ideal for decoupage.

Tyler is a Spiderman fan. So, bingo, I will decoupage his chest of drawers and give them a theme of everyone's favourite friendly neighbourhood Spiderman. What a mammoth task this turned into; I was cutting, gluing, and varnishing every day for the entirety of my Christmas holidays. I wanted it to be perfect, so I planned and stayed focused with patience and consistency. Some days I didn't feel like decoupaging, but I stayed true to my intention and goal. I wanted it finished by the time I went back to work.

And I did it! I was so happy, and so was he. You can see a video and pictures of my decoupaging prowess on my Facebook page. I felt as though I had accomplished something. Looking back now, I realise that I actually applied some key elements of the mindset I had been building in my recovery to complete this project. Planning, preparation, focus, patience, consistency, motivation, and determination. Everything was coming together.

We can find new passions, new focus, through activities such as crafts. We can begin to open new doorways of opportunity for ourselves. We all have something that can make us feel good. During my recovery, I have learnt that I enjoy writing and turning my hand to decoupage – something I would not have realised had I not started on this journey. Tyler would still have his shabby old chest of drawers, and this book would not have been written. We do not know what we can accomplish until we actually start something and are prepared to go all the way.

I strongly recommend learning a craft like decoupage to practise during trigger times. The feeling of reward when you have completed your project is amazing. It is a fantastic way of making us aware of what we can do when we set our mind to something and stick to it. Check out the photos and videos on my Facebook page and the chapter on trigger time activities for decoupaging instructions.

18. Trigger Time Activities and Mindset Exercises

Arts and crafts are awesome things to get into during our trigger times and in the quiet moments between group meetings or counselling sessions. During idle moments, we are more susceptible to our triggers and cravings. So I believe that taking up a craft or hobby can help you through those difficult times.

Why? Crafting assists us in many ways that can be applied to recovery. Most crafts and arts require focus, consistency, and patience – three key elements that will strengthen our mindset, which will aid significantly in staying sober and working towards an alcohol-free life.

Crafting is a positive, productive activity that will also provide you with a feeling of accomplishment. This can offer a gentle lift and help us regain the sense of pride we may have lost while caught in the whirlpool of addiction.

There are loads of different crafts to try, and the only way you will find out if you like doing something is by taking that step, dipping your toe, and having a go. If you're unsure of what to try, think back to when you were younger. Was there an activity you felt especially drawn to but never attempted? Perhaps there was a craft you used to partake in, but your practice fell by the wayside as your addiction worsened. Well, maybe it's time you picked up your knitting needles once more, dipped your pen, or tuned that guitar!

The possibilities are endless. You may ignite new or old passions during your recovery period with consistency, which would be fantastic.

For me, it was decoupage and writing, as we discussed earlier. I would like to share with you how I decoupage for you to try. Maybe your itch to get crafting is with something else? Have a think and get started! You never know until you try.

How to Decoupage

In order to decoupage successfully, you need patience and attention. Focus is the name of the game, and by indulging in a little decoupage, we are also practising being mindful and we probably don't even realise it. It is a great activity to help us get through those difficult periods when we lack stimuli and can very easily lapse or fall by the wayside.

Okay, Get Busy …

First you need an item to decoupage. This can be anything, ideally with a smooth surface. I did Tyler's chest of drawers over Christmas, which was a mammoth task. For your first few attempts, I would do something small like a picture frame or a mirror. You don't want to go for something too ambitious, struggle, and then throw in the towel. Also, don't practise on something of huge value to you. I don't want you feeling devastated that you destroyed something of great value to you or someone else. Charity shops are a great place to source items to upcycle, as are boot fairs. You have your item and now you're going to need some equipment.

Tools for the Job ...

Scissors

Craft knife or a Stanley

Brushes (I try to have a selection of sizes) – good ones; you don't want hairs dropping out and ruining your masterpiece!

A small roller or similar to smooth out bubbles

A soft sponge

A rag

Decoupage glue – personally I will only use Mod Podge. There are many types of glue available. Some people just use bog standard PVA glue, which works fine, but for me, the best I've found for the types of things I upcycle is Mod Podge by far.

You can get Mod Podge in many different types – glossy, glitter, matte, etc. It's really down to personal taste and the look you're trying to get for the specific project.

Clear varnish – I personally use yacht varnish.

Type of Paper

Again, this comes down to personal choice and what you're trying to make. Most of my items are made from comics that are destined for the comic graveyard. As a comic collector, I stumble across these from time to time and save them for my decoupage.

PLEASE BE AWARE IF YOU USE COMICS, CHECK THE COMIC FIRST – YOU COULD BE DESTROYING SOMETHING SPECIAL, AND MY HEART WILL CRY!

I personally do not like using paper with a glossy finish. You can use tissue paper, wallpaper, wrapping paper, or you can print images from a computer if you have a good laser printer.

Prepare Your Area ...

I am an incredibly messy worker, so I've learnt over the years to put cloths down and wear old clothes. I've ruined so many T-shirts with varnish over the years, it's unreal.

Prepare Your Item ...

I like to have a plan in mind, and I cut the images I want and place them where I would like them to be before I start gluing.

I then take a photo because I'm getting old and my memory is naff, and I take them off in order, so that when I put them back on, they will be in sequence.

Personally, I cut smaller pieces rather than use whole pages, as it runs less risk of bubbles.

Step One ...

You can decoupage on many things – wood, glass, plastic, etc. But it is important to have a surface that is as smooth as possible. For a first attempt, I would recommend something small like a jewellery box, money box, picture frame, or simply a plain square piece of wood to practise on.

Try to make sure your items have limited chips or bumps, preferably none.

Clean the surface, making it free from dust, etc.

Step Two ...

Now we start! I brush a thin layer of glue over the surface area where I will place my first image.

Step Three ...

I place the image over the area and flatten it out in one direction, smoothing out the bubbles. I then take my roller and go over the image.

Step Four ...

Mop up any runaway glue with the soft sponge.

Step Five ...

I repeat the process, moving around the item with my sequence of images. I often overlap images to hide any areas of the original surface.

Step Six ...

Once all the images are in place and I am happy, I then cover with a coat of Mod Podge. Personally, I like to give three coats of Mod Podge. Make certain the item is dry before applying another coat, which is normally around 30–40 minutes depending on the project.

Step Seven ...

As you build up more layers, you will begin to see your item getting a new lease of life! Now sit back, relax, and gaze upon your creation with pride. Go to bed and continue the next day.

Step Eight ...

You have got up, you have checked out Year One for some inspiration and a kick up the bum, and now you're excited to get varnishing! How many coats of varnish you will need really depends on your item.

I normally do at least two. Tyler's chest of drawers took four coats. You will have to be the judge.

I normally leave a good few hours between coats of varnish.

Step Nine ...

You're all done! Easy, wasn't it? And you kept yourself busy for a few days doing something positive and productive. The final step is to take some photos and send them to me at the Facebook page with a message to big yourself up and show me your creation.

Step Ten ...

Now it's time to move on, get creative, and pretty soon you'll be hunting round the charity shops wanting to decoupage everything ... you are limited only by your imagination!

Other Things to Try

Get proactive in your own recovery, and during those trigger times, keep busy with a positive, productive activity. You can try:

- Exercising
- Cooking
- Writing
- Crafting
- Learning an instrument
- Gardening
- Gaming

I decided to get proactive in my recovery, and now I'm asking you to do the same!

Here are some mindset exercises I've also completed for you to try. A quick Google search will reveal lots of other activities for you. We are all different, as are our personal journeys.

19. Rewrite the Story of Your Life

On the evening of my eighth day sober, I decided to complete this exercise, which is great for your mindset. When it gets to the evening, I often begin to crave alcohol, normally between the hours of 18:00 and 21:00.

I know that doesn't sound long, but you would be amazed at the damage I can do at this time of day. To counter this, I have been trying to be productive by conducting small exercises that may offer some assistance on my road to recovery and sobriety.

This was the first exercise I tried. It's a fantastic exercise where you visualise the life that you want as if it were already in existence. This offers you a positive focus on attaining your goals.

There is a famous saying that if you can see it in your mind, you can hold it in your hand!

This saying very much encapsulates this small but powerful exercise.

Once you can picture the life you want as if you are living it now, write this story down on paper. Be as detailed as you like; write what you see directly on the paper as if it is your life right now.

Focus ...

Take your time ...

Really be there ...

You can take your time and even complete it over the course of a few days – there's no rush! This is your story – you want to get it right. Once you put pen to paper, this is the first time your hopes and dreams are coming from your mind and your heart into the physical world. Now the universe has something physical that it can work with, and it will begin to work with you!

Once you have done this, put the story somewhere you can see it often to remind you. When you see it, believe that this is your life. You are sober! You are clean! You are strong!

Letting Go of the Past

Sharon told me about a practice that helps us let go of situations, circumstances, and people that have had such an impact on us that we stay tied to the negative emotions or trauma that we have experienced. This in turn has a knock-on effect on our behaviour in the present moment.

I have been through many traumatic experiences; however, there are three that reoccur to me time and time again. When I am drunk, they always seem to return, and at night, when I struggle to sleep, they pop into my mind.

The first is my mother leaving me and my brother when I was a baby. When I finally found my mum, she had been dead for a year. I had looked for her for most of my adult life (although my family was unaware), and when I found her, I still never got the closure I needed. I can hear from other people why she left … but that is just hearsay. I needed to hear it from her.

The second is that I was sexually abused for a number of years and it never came out until after the guy killed himself, when I was a young man serving in the armed forces. My family never acknowledged it or spoke with me about it.

The third is the death of my son Joseph. He died of anencephaly after nine months of hell. Feeling my baby kick and knowing he was going to die tore me apart. My then wife wouldn't let me go to his wake because of my past mistakes with alcohol. I drove from London to Kent and cried the whole way, alone; my life fell apart. I couldn't even sit with my daughter because of my alcoholism.

These are the three key moments that I felt, when I put pen to paper, I needed to allow myself to move on from.

The Exercise to Cut the Ties

I decided to give this exercise a go. You write a letter to the past person, situation, or circumstance. This is a very personal letter. I took a great deal of time over each one and allowed myself to tell each person my feelings – how I felt then and how I am now ready to move forward.

I found this a very emotional experience but also a great exercise to allow me to begin the unloading process, lifting the weight from my shoulders.

By putting pen to paper and writing my emotions down, addressing each situation, I also found this empowering. I was finally letting out the thoughts and feelings that I had kept to myself for so long.

Guilt

Anger

A sense of loss

Confusion

Remorse

Grief

Shame

To name just a few.

Handing Over to the Universe

Once I had my letters, I needed to hand them over to the universe, to pass my burdens on and release myself from the past so that I could look forward with greater confidence and clarity.

There are many ways you can do this. I decided to have myself a small ritual alone, outside, where I burnt each letter. In my mind I felt that the words would be carried up with the smoke into the ether, where the spirit of each person would receive my words.

But perhaps more than that, I felt that seeing the smoke being carried up and the letters disintegrating in the flame had significant symbolism to me. It physically showed me that this was now done.

And I did feel a sense of release.

Still a Long Road to Go ...

I knew that I still had a long way to go, but I felt more comfortable discussing these situations. I had finally unlocked the areas of my past that had had such a huge emotional impact on me and, in doing so, I had also broken the chains that kept me tied to them and stopped me from moving forward.

21 Days Sober Challenge

I found this exercise that I completed on Day 21 alcohol-free both rewarding and eye-opening. The 21 Days Sober Challenge is an exercise that gets us to recognise all that we have to be grateful for in life. So what is the challenge? Well, when you get to 21 days, list 21 things about your life that you are grateful for. Many people find it easy to reel off the first five or six, but once we go above that, we really do need to start focusing on ourselves, both inwardly and outwardly.

You can spend the whole day on this challenge in the back of your mind, and I discovered that the deeper I looked, the more profound were the reasons to be grateful – more than I had ever expected, which gave me confidence in my recovery journey. It also made me aware of my reasons to continue being sober, as well as the various means of support that I may otherwise have forgotten about.

Give it a go at your 21-day point and you will be surprised at what there is to be grateful for if you really look within your heart and give this challenge the attention that it deserves.

20. Living with an Addict

This section of the book I dedicate to my partner Sharon's thoughts, feelings, and experiences of living with an addict. She has experienced living with someone struggling with alcoholism from two perspectives: first as my partner of over eleven years and second with her father, so she can share her experiences of being the child of an alcoholic parent and the partner of an alcoholic.

I asked Sharon to write some articles for the Facebook page giving her perspective. I admit, these were very difficult for me to read, and when I did, I was bombarded with a range of feelings – largely guilt, shame, and horror at how my behaviour had made the woman I love feel. Yes, they were difficult for me to read, but I know that as I have spent a large amount of my recovery owning my shit, I needed to know exactly how my alcoholism had affected those closest to me. This was an eye-opener for me. As an alcoholic addict, I never wanted to hurt anyone intentionally, but I was too focused on myself and my need for alcohol to see the damage that I was doing to her. A by-product of my alcoholism was the mental despair I was causing her and others in my life.

These are the articles she wrote for the page.

Living with an Addict: Part One

I look at myself and see a human being who lost her light, a light that dimmed over the years without me noticing.

Looking in the mirror, I asked myself 'Who am I without the addict?' and I really couldn't answer. I think it's fair to say that I built an illusion that I presented to others which was far from the reality that I experienced.

I opened my front door every day with the pretence that my life was without its problems when, in fact, Matt was struggling with his inner demons that could make life unbearable at times. Little moments like cuddling each other as we went to sleep were stripped away by his PTSD, which left me fearful that if I accidentally scared him in his sleep, he may kill me in the heat of the moment.

Enjoying a meal in a restaurant sometimes triggered his paranoia to the point where he would usher me out in a frenzy before the food came. At the same time, onlookers sniggered at his behaviour, not knowing that his PTSD had surfaced. Weekends became a time that I dreaded, as I knew the binge drinking would start, often resulting in arguments where the hurtful words chipped at my very being and damaged the confidence I had in myself.

Family and friend gatherings became less and less, as I wanted to hide the reality that Matt could not control his drinking. When he drank, his demons surfaced and a different person emerged.

It became routine on weekends to start drinking after the kids went to bed, argue all night, and then apologise the following day.

Addicts blame their substance for their behaviour and hide behind it and never truly take responsibility for their actions, which have lasting effects on the person who has to endure the environment they find themselves in. Forgiveness became a large part of our relationship, but forgetting is not easy.

As the years went on, I isolated myself, became depressed and disconnected from my true self. I didn't trust anyone enough to open up to them or seek help, mainly because I didn't want anyone to look at Matt differently from the person they knew and loved. I knew deep down that he could not satisfy the demons that swirled inside his head, and turning to alcohol eased his pain. In turn, I ended up sacrificing my own wellbeing and became a person I didn't recognise anymore.

Matt had many personalities over the years, and it felt like I was in a new relationship every few years – the hippy, the vegetarian, the squaddie, the fitness freak, the shaman, to mention but a few – but one thing was consistent … alcohol.

I had to adjust myself to suit each character, love each character, and understand his need to change himself to mask his pain. The hungry ghost couldn't see what value he had at the present moment. Always wanting something better, an illusion created to satisfy himself for a short period. This left me an outsider, always feeling like I wasn't good enough … Why aren't I good enough? Why can't he just stop drinking? What can I do to make him happy? These are questions we ask ourselves, as we think the problem lies with ourselves rather than the addict.

Why didn't I leave? is the question many ask; the answer isn't as black and white as many think. Matt is 30 per cent dickhead, but the other 70 per cent is a good man and a good father who will do anything for his family. His light far outshines the 30 per cent of darkness that he has buried within his soul.

It's easy for people to say that you should leave, but how can you walk out on a person you love who has endured so much in their life when their only downfall is not being able to reach out and get the help they need?

No one can ever understand the turmoil we have within ourselves about our decisions unless they have drowned on the same ship. The year 2020 has been challenging for most people, but for me, it has been a year of self-reflection and being forced to find myself again. At the beginning of the year, I tried to think back to when I was truly happy. When did I last feel safe and loved and have inner peace?

This took me to a time when I was spiritually connected to my spirit helpers, when I believed that I was worthy of being loved and worthy of being happy. A time when I put myself first and had self-love. I started asking the universe to take me back to that happy place. I yearned to rewind time and find that Sharon again.

Overnight, Matt made the decision to move out and we went into lockdown. I found myself alone, a single mum and trapped with no one but myself for company. I remember thinking *FFS … this isn't exactly what I asked the universe for,* but I had to trust that I needed it. Matt was on his own journey, and I moved forward with mine.

I took little steps to re-find my connection to my spirit helpers, dug out my 'Healing with Fairies' cards, and took the advice I was given. It wasn't easy at first, as I had to give my trust back to the universe and allow it to burn my life to the ground. One of the first cards I drew indicated that I needed a vacation: *lol yeah, right*, I thought, *lockdown will allow me a holiday*. Still, upon reflection, I realised my mind needed a holiday – a break from worrying about how to make others happy.

A clear mind was needed away from worries about being alone, employment, finances, lockdown, and what was happening in the world around me, so I used my yoga sessions to find silence and quieten my mind from the rush of worries that clouded my days. The second card that stood out to me was 'being honest with myself and people around me'. This card was very significant for the changes I made in my life.

As I started opening up to my friends, it became apparent that they listened without judgement and were more supportive than I would ever have imagined. The burden I carried was instantly taken away. I don't want to go too much into detail about my beliefs, as many follow a different path. Still, no matter your beliefs, the message you must take is that you need to look after yourself, love yourself, and take steps to heal yourself.

Healing yourself will allow you to help others. If you have a hole in your lifeboat, you cannot help anyone else, as you will end up drowning yourself and the people you're trying to help. Do little things each day for yourself; look at yourself in the mirror each morning and tell yourself that you deserve happiness and believe that the universe will bring that for you. Don't think about how it will be brought to you; just trust with your whole heart that it will.

I have a little ritual that I do for myself. I go into a quiet place, close my eyes, and talk about all the things that don't bring me happiness. I visualise these problems in my hands, and then I throw them into the universe. I ask the universe to take care of them, as I do not want to think about them anymore. Trust and believe that you deserve better. This will attract new life opportunities, bringing healing.

Healing doesn't happen overnight. It isn't always brought to you the way you want. Sometimes lighting a match and watching everything you know burn to the ground is what it takes for something new to grow.

Listen to your gut and trust that the universe has your back.

I no longer think *am I good enough?* Of course I am good enough. I have lived through some of the most challenging times and I am still standing, stronger than I ever was. You are the magician, and within your grasp are the amazing forces of earth and spirit.

You are the alchemist of your life and able to transform your difficulties into great blessings. Reclaim your power and embrace your intentions in your heart and in your daily life. Looking back over the last decade of my life, I realise that I am stronger than I thought.

Living with an Addict: Part Two

Another year has gone by, and what a year it has been. 2020 was a year of reflection. The universe held a mirror up to me, and I was forced to look back at past events and how they influenced me into being the person I was.

This took me back to my childhood. My father was a high-functioning alcoholic who drank from the minute his eyes opened to the world until he passed out on his pillow at night. Normal people would reach for their coffee as a source of 'wake me up', but my dad reached for brandy (which was his choice of drink). He worked for Eskom in South Africa on the power lines for most of his life. This very intelligent man fooled many people around him – or maybe he didn't, and people just chose not to see.

My dad was an abusive, violent man who could not control his temper; it was worse the more he drank. I am a person who can see through the masks that people wear to hide their true selves. Still, I learnt from a very young age that it was not beneficial for me to call him out on his BS but better to stand in the shadows away from his wrath, which fell upon us regularly.

My memories of my dad are probably very different from those of my siblings, as I was definitely not the favourite child. I was the child who didn't fall for the 'sorry, I did it because I love you' or 'I'm sorry, but if you just behaved, I wouldn't have to do this' routine, and although I didn't voice it, my face and body language struggled to hide my growing hatred for a man who I was meant to love.

There are a few memories that have stuck with me all my life. These events carved out the distorted view I have of appreciation, self-love, and acceptable boundaries.

We learn what 'love' is from the people who 'love' us. How are we to know that what we experience as 'love' is not actually the love we deserve? Love is a learned behaviour.

Self-love: One of my memories that affected me most was that my dad rarely called me by my name.

He always referred to me as 'Deiwels se kind' (those who don't understand Afrikaans, the translation is 'Devil's child'). As a child, this became my identity. The seed was planted that I came from a dark place – someone who was not worthy of friendship or love.

On the rare occasions when I would bring friends home, my father would make comments like 'I am surprised a lovely child like you would be friends with the Devil's child' while swigging his brandy and struggling to stay steady on his feet.

The embarrassment and shame would wash over me like a wave that I had underestimated and leave me drowning under its crushing weight. I, of course, laughed it off, but each time it was said, it was another chip taken from my self-worth.

Although I had many 'friends' while at school, I did not form any solid connections or attachments. They were acquaintances who never got the chance to see the inner demons that plagued me.

I distanced myself from having real connections with the people around me. I closed myself off from ever experiencing 'real love'. It took me a long time to free myself from this label that my dad suffocated me with for many years.

I now see that he inadvertently called himself the Devil, and I was indeed the Devil's child, and this was no reflection on me as a person.

Appreciation: Although a drunk, my dad was a stickler for appreciation and manners. These values were taught to us through mental and physical abuse.

I remember going on holiday and the hotel had a buffet breakfast. *Yum*, I thought and took a little bit of everything they had to offer. At the same time, my dad watched me from a distance.

As I sat down at the table ready to tuck in, my dad said, 'You are greedy, and you had better eat what you have taken.' As I begin to eat, I started to fill up with dread, as I knew I would not be able to finish what was on my plate.

My dad knew this and sat watching me in silence; when my mum and siblings were done with their food and ready to go, my dad said the dreaded words 'We aren't going anywhere until she finishes her food.' I sat at that table for hours, crying and gagging while trying to force myself to eat what was left on my plate while onlookers stood around feeling sorry for me.

My dad would not give in. He had no compassion and felt no guilt. I sat at that table for what seemed like an eternity until I ate every crumb on my plate. By the time we got down to the beach, my dad was three sheets to the wind and I was a snivelling wreck who just wanted to hide from the world.

The day ended with my dad being pulled out of the sea by lifeguards with his swimming trunks around his ankles. As I watched each wave crash on him while he struggled to stand under their weight, I had a moment where I wished he had drowned.

Like many other incidents of this kind with my dad, this event crushed my spirit, and I became submissive in my dealings with others, avoided confrontation, and accepted behaviour that I thought was acceptable.

Appreciate what you have and don't take more than you need – that's what my dad taught me; a distorted view that I don't deserve more than what I need.

Don't spend money on those expensive shoes; you don't need them. Don't strive to be more than you can be because you should appreciate where you are. Don't expect more love than someone is willing to give; appreciate what little love they can give you … bollocks.

One thing 2020 has taught me is that I always deserve more – more love, more friends, more hugs, more openness, and more communication … and yes, I do deserve those shoes! Even though Matt bought them for me, I wear them with pride because I am worth it.

During my childhood and teenage years, I could not understand why it took my mum so long to leave. Still, through my own experience, I now understand the strength it takes to change patterns and learned behaviours.

You have to dig deep within yourself to realise that you are worth so much more, and it takes courage to make the changes necessary to give yourself a fighting chance.

Finding self-love is not selfish. It is not self-indulgent. It is a significant value that children need to learn and feel from a young age. We are important, we are worth it, and we deserve to be heard and loved.

Had I learnt this valuable lesson as a child, I may not have lost my self-worth.

It will take me some time to find my voice, but I am learning to love myself and appreciate every part of my being … one day at a time.

At the age of forty-two, the universe gave me a kick up the bum. It was time to let go of the toxic memories that plagued my life and kept me chained to negative patterns. I now give myself permission to be true to myself.

Living with an Addict: Part Three

As the new year began, I was full of motivation. I started de-cluttering the house and started in the kitchen. I was cleaning out one of the cupboards. As I stretched my hand around an unseen section, I could feel an empty bottle. My heart sank and a wave of anxiety flowed through my body.

As I sat on the floor, my mind was taken back to all the empty bottles that had been hidden around the house over the years. *I have only had three cans* … but the other twelve were shoved into nooks and crannies that I didn't know existed. The feeling of dread filled me as I braved it, pulling out the bottle to see it.

As I pulled it out, relief sprang from every pore … it was mine.

My relief quickly changed to embarrassment and shame; although I am not a big drinker, I had resorted to hiding wine. Matt decided to stop drinking, and I wanted to support him.

In support, I gave up this pleasure myself. Matt works long hours and is sometimes away from home. One of those nights, I decided to have some wine after a long day. There was some left in the bottle. I quickly shoved it into the cupboard before Matt arrived home, and I hid the fact that I had indulged in a relaxed moment when I was alone at home.

I'd forgotten it was there, but I had to ask myself *why did I hide it?*

This got me thinking about the sacrifices we make when living with an addict. Besides a glass of wine, which is a small sacrifice in support of a recovering addict, I looked at my life, starting as a child. I wrote down all the sacrifices I had made to survive someone else's addiction.

Memories swirled through my mind – memories that took away little pieces of me until I became submissive and put the addicts' happiness above my own. I sacrificed my words the most and silently retreated into my own inner world.

Living with an addict, you learn to pick your battles to stay out of harm's way. Little by little, each day, you suppress your words. You accept the frequent apologies by smiling silently. Still, inside, your heart is crumbling at the cruel and callous behaviour that comes from someone you love.

Your honest thoughts remain in your head, swirling around like demons that constantly taunt you. Did they mean those horrid things they said or did?

Was it the drink, or did the drink draw out their actual perception of me?

Am I to blame?

What can I do to make them happy?

How can I change myself?

Am I such a bad person that the universe thought I deserved this life?

My words failed to communicate the damage these behaviours caused me throughout my life. My silence kept me from harm and drew me into the darkness of self-hate.

Self-doubt and lack of confidence filled every corner of my mind like a dark shadow. I was chained to my negative thoughts.

I couldn't speak out about any areas of my life that made me unhappy. I became accustomed to being silent, and my thoughts became my best friend.

I now understand 'healthy mind, healthy body' … I certainly did not have a healthy mind for a long time. I stored negative energy and thoughts within my mind, which led to weight gain. The weight gain led to low confidence and increased negative thoughts.

It's a vicious circle that traps you and leaves you feeling helpless and unloved. I am ashamed to admit that I became an empty shell. Many people can relate to this, even if they don't live with an addict.

'We tend to take care of what we love, and maybe that is why so few of us take care of ourselves.'

These words have stuck in my mind over the last few months, a reminder that I, too, am important.

At the end of 2019, my turning point was when the darkness was at its worst. The kids had grown up and flown the nest. The only unconditional love I had was spreading its wings and making its own way in life.

I was isolated in a place I didn't want to be, and I had an overwhelming feeling of not wanting to be in this world anymore. I was no longer needed.

As the words came tumbling out of my mouth, I expected the same compassion and empathy I had given others through the years. Instead, I was met with hostility.

In that moment, I realised that even though I had spent my life uplifting others, having compassion for circumstances, and understanding unacceptable behaviour, I can give someone the world and, in return, not have a place in it.

I broke myself trying to heal others, and now I had to pick up the pieces and put myself back together.

It has been a difficult process to learn real self-love, to look at yourself in the mirror each day and be proud of who you are and how much inner strength you have.

Look back on your sacrifices and find the positives that came from them. Your sacrifices were not weaknesses. Wrap your arms around yourself and give yourself a big hug. Love yourself the way you deserve to be loved, and changes will begin.

21. A Family in Recovery

Sharon never gave up on me through all the pain I caused, and all my nan ever wanted was for me to be happy. All my kids needed was for me to be there and not in the abyss, comforted by alcohol. All my heart wanted was to be heard, but it was weakened by my addictions and drowned out by the voices of my demons.

It is not just the drinker who suffers when alcohol becomes a problem. Our families and loved ones are also suffering, caught within a battle from which they often cannot see any release. I know I hurt many loved ones over the years through my drinking and drug-taking. But at the time, I couldn't see it. Being caught within that cycle, I was lost in the haze of selfishness that alcoholism and addiction creates.

It is important to remember that although we enter recovery for ourselves, we are also improving the lives of the people we love and care about. By breaking the cycle, you will strengthen your circle.

I know in my heart that many of the bridges I burnt may be unrepairable, and I understand that now. My focus is on what I can do to ensure I build new bridges and solid foundations so that I can learn from my mistakes and failings and not condemn myself to a life sentence.

Realisation and acceptance are crucial to moving forward. Realise and accept that your problem is, in many cases, your family's problem too, and from that point, make the changes you need to while you can.

If you can look in the mirror and be honest with yourself, you have begun a new journey towards healing yourself, and of that, you should be proud.

Reading Sharon's perspective and understanding what I have put her through over the years really brought things home to me. Just as I have had to heal the wounds of my past, I know Sharon will also be going through her own healing process.

Addiction goes far deeper than what we see on the surface, which is influenced by what society dictates and others' views or opinions.

Learning to heal from my past has been one of the key elements in my recovery. This has also taught me a great deal when I look at myself and others. Facing my past was something I always feared.

One day I stood in court and thought I was going to jail for violent disorder and causing affray. Another day I went to a clinic to be tested for HIV and other STIs, just in case the Predator had left me with one final farewell scar. (I was okay, thank God.) These are just some of the ever-present memories I struggled with from my childhood and throughout my adult life. But I was utterly unaware that I was continually pushing the self-destruct button by suppressing such instances and burying them deep.

People do not see these memories – only I do – so how can they understand and how can I expect them to? Although I was the addict and Sharon the supportive partner, we are both in recovery from addiction. That is clear to me now.

The power of communication, connection, compassion, and understanding is so strong, as is the importance of reaching out to others for help and support and explaining how we feel within ourselves.

All my life, I felt ashamed, damaged, dirty, anxious, angry, and sad, to name but a few, at the hand I had been dealt. I never expressed this, so I reached for the safety net of escape through solvents, drugs, and alcohol. A short-term fix to forget, but one that caused long-term problems in my life.

Perhaps if I had opened up to Sharon sooner, things would not have got so bad that I pulled her under with me. But hindsight is a beautiful thing, and to be honest, it won't help us move forward as a family; communication will.

22. Final Thought for Year One

It's never too late.

Being a role model is the most potent form of education we can offer to our younger generations. Our children are great imitators, so it is vitally important to give them something truly amazing to imitate. But it is not only the young who take inspiration from others.

The pathway you decide to take and the changes you begin to make will inspire those you encounter throughout your life, and you may not even realise it. But to do so, we must first learn to be true to ourselves.

I like to think that I need to be the role model I needed when I was young. Our words matter and our actions matter.

As humans, we look to each other for inspiration daily, so being a role model really isn't optional. But the role model we choose to be is!

It's never too late to turn things around and never too late to show those we encounter or our children integrity, love, honesty, and compassion. Never too late to show our strengths and accept our weaknesses and to demonstrate that we did not give up when things got tough.

It's never too late to show people that it's okay to fall and it's okay to make mistakes, but it is how we respond that can teach the greatest of lessons. Be the person you were born to be and the role model you need to be!

Since Christmas 2020, my recovery has come on tenfold. Facing up to such a difficult challenge on the back of losing three family members earlier in the year, I know I have the strength to keep going and live the life I want to – the authentic life I was born to have.

Facing up to these challenges were massive turning points for me. Now I feel confident in moving forward and have the tools I need to successfully combat my addictions and my childhood traumas. Opening up and sharing my past experiences has been like lifting a heavy weight from my shoulders.

I sleep well now without the need for any substances. I openly talk about my experiences with anyone who wants to hear them, to demonstrate that it is okay to speak out. The shame is not on the survivor but on the abuser.

Today my world is good. The last year had its difficulties, but the victories far outweigh the struggles. This makes me feel confident that I can move forward with a sober mind and a happy heart. I am encouraged to explore the world's possibilities and share them with my family, breaking the cycle and building new memories. Recovery is not easy, and I am so proud of anyone willing to step up and make changes within their lives, no matter what those changes are.

Having the courage to stop and say to ourselves 'enough is enough' can be one of the hardest things we can do. Seeing those changes through to the end brings forth new challenges and difficulties that can feel scary at times, which is natural. We always tend to fear the unknown, which all too often forces us to stick to the same old roads and worn-out pathways where nothing changes and everything stays the same.

But if you can lift your head up and see the other available roads, if you can take those first few steps towards them, reaching out for support where it is needed and working hard to clear the road ahead of all its obstacles and debris one brick at a time ... if you can do so with consistency and discipline, then you can accomplish – you can succeed. You will come out the other side as a survivor and a winner.

I just have one favour to ask you, and that is when you come out the other side and find your way, please reach back and help others out of the whirlpool of addiction. Learn to listen, empathise, and understand. Offer support where it is needed and do all you can to lift one another up. The world would be so much easier if we all gave each other a helping hand from time to time – if we took a moment to stop and listen to each other's stories and what led them to this present moment in time.

Those who have suffered childhood trauma and people struggling with addiction are some of our society's most vulnerable members. It's time we learned to listen without judgement. Hopefully, we can all be encouraged to say the words ...

I can't speak for tomorrow, and I'm not focused on yesterday, but today I'm not drinking.

Just a thought.

23. Reflections of a Broken Mirror

These are some of my thoughts that I journaled at different stages during my first 100 days of recovery. I'd like to share them with you. When I write my reflections, I try not to overthink about the content but instead allow the words to flow from my heart.

The Choice

After years of failure and setbacks in my battle against alcohol, I finally made the choice to begin my road to recovery, and I can tell you now, I was damn certain in the decision that this would be my final attempt and I would crack it! The very next day, I relapsed. I was again caged by the circle that had kept me chained to the floor, never being able to move forward and progress as a normal functioning member of society; nope, I was forever to be a piss head.

This is the deep sense of failure I felt that day. I had given it all the big talk; 'I'm never drinking again,' blah blah blah. Stuff my partner Sharon had heard a million times before. I do feel now, looking back, that that was my first mistake, the big talk. Setting the humongous goal of never drinking again when I had barely been sober twelve hours. I was setting myself up to fail. I've now been sober eleven days and I'm feeling pretty good, but I have steered clear of setting the big goal of NEVER DRINKING AGAIN IN MY LIFE! EVER!

Instead, now I focus on one day at a time. *Just get through today, Matt* or *I'm not going to drink today ... I don't know what will happen tomorrow, but for today, I'm not drinking.* I have been finding that this mode of thought has kept me more conscious in my decision-making and the choices that I make for my recovery from alcohol. I find that by allowing myself to have this mindset, I am more present in my decision-making, which in turn gives me more power or control over my alcoholism.

I am not saying that this is easy … oh, no, no, no! I have wobbled and will no doubt wobble again very soon. When my guard is down, the drunkard demon comes a-whispering in my ear, and I often feel that on his way there, he has knocked out the sober angel, who I need whispering in the other ear, because nine times out of ten he falls silent and I'm left with the demon and his pathetic reasons that he gives me, like … it's okay for me to drink.

Or other statements such as *you wanna be like every other bloke, don't you? How are you going to enjoy yourself? You've worked hard all week! Have a couple; it won't hurt! Everyone loves you once you've had a drink … you're so much fun!* And many more, but I'm sure you get the idea. So, yes, it is not easy and it is a constant battle – one I do feel I'm winning at the moment, but I am not getting overconfident just yet. This is not my first rodeo, and I have been here before. The one thing that I feel is different this time is the choice I made. It's that first step and true acknowledgement of where you are right now and what needs to be done that's important. By setting that intention with solidity and by having no doubts, I believe it's a point we can all reach in time – when enough is enough and we make that solid choice for real.

So if you relapse or have relapsed recently, please don't let it set you back. Maybe your mindset was not right at that time. You can get there, and the time will come when something will click within and an inner knowledge will tell you *now, this time, you got this!* Sure, it will still take willpower, self-discipline, an open mind, and a willingness to hold up a mirror to yourself and really desire that change. But we can all get there! I still have a long way to go, believe me, but I'm not focusing on the end of my journey or where I want to get to. All I'm focusing on is this exact moment in time, the only moment I have power over, and in this moment, I'm saying *no thanks, I don't want a drink. Not today.*

Identity

As I began to look deeper into my journey through life leading up to these last eighty days of clarity, I found myself looking through old photos and realised the staggering changes I had made in regards to my outlook, personality, and the way I wanted to be perceived by the world.

Many of these changes seemed quite drastic. I would change from year to year or month to month, but I was never able to carry any consistency or happiness within myself. I simply moved through cycles of different versions of myself.

Of course, as I look at these and ponder to myself, I think that since the sexual abuse that I endured when I was younger over the course of around six years and the unprovoked attack that nearly killed me, I had not been an authentic version of myself.

What I mean is that I tried to find happiness in being someone else. Inside, I was hurting, but I could never display this, as I simply never spoke about it. I also felt uneasy approaching anyone and discussing what had happened to me. Would I be thought of as dirty? Would people view me as the pervert or question my sexuality?

This, among many other things, kept the feelings and the pain locked inside me. Now I'm older and wish to share my story, looking back, I feel I hid the real me away and looked for a different version of myself, if that makes sense. So I regularly changed my appearance, my circle of friends, my hobbies and interests, in many cases my complete personality! I lived a very large amount of my adult life as someone else.

As many different Matts, never showing my true authentic self, I did not love myself. Inside, I felt ashamed, and, in many ways, this led to the imminent setting of the self-destruct button ready to be pushed. I felt I had – somewhere in the world – a mum who didn't want me.

A predator used me for sexual gratification, I didn't fit in with my family, and I was attacked and left for dead for no reason whatsoever. All by the time I was thirteen years old! No wonder, as I got older, I looked to be anyone other than myself. Of course, partly because of not speaking out and finding support, I drank and took drugs to find comfort and ease the pain – sometimes just so that I could sleep at night, so I wouldn't have to close my eyes and replay events over and over.

I was inflicting further pain on myself but I was unaware, coasting along, fuelling the rocket that was aimed directly at the tempting self-destruct button. Now I can see this, and, through sharing my story, I am finally beginning to peel off the layers of pain that have formed the many characters I have played throughout my life.

I feel a sense of freedom and that, yes, the real Matt, the little boy who loved planes and longed to fly, is rotating back to face the world again! I guess what I am trying to say, my friend, is this: love yourself enough to live your truth. I lost many years of myself to alcohol and drugs, violence, upset, and anger, largely because I was too afraid to speak out when I was screaming inside.

The Why

While sitting here in my hotel jotting down notes, I began to wonder. Although I went through a series of traumas at a young age and very close together, why did this lead to alcoholism and addiction?

I like to ask myself questions like this from time to time, when I can give it some thought and generate good honest responses. My feeling is that it's because I was fed alcohol at a young age by my abuser. Although I had been around alcohol my whole life, my abuser drip fed it to me so that he could have his piece of pie later on. But what I am realising is that the alcohol did cause a series of side effects which I feel got carried through to later life. I would pass out faster so the night would be over quicker.

The alcohol would numb me; I would feel no pain or discomfort. The next day, there was a very good chance I would not remember everything. Often, though, I would just pretend I couldn't remember, lying to myself to protect myself. So I suppose alcohol, solvents, and drugs became an armour for me, a protective shield.

Alcohol offered me comfort and security but more notably an escape. With this in mind, as I grew older, it becomes easy for me to understand why, then, whenever I faced difficulties, fears, anxieties, and challenges, I would turn to my liquid bodyguard. When I faced troubles, I wanted them over quickly. When I felt pain, I wanted to be numbed. When I experienced trauma, I wanted to forget. And when things really got bad, I had to escape!

Because this programming had become my normal behaviour pattern at the hands of my abuser, it also became my one constant in adult life. I am glad that now I can think about these things with a positive mind. Please be aware that I'm not dwelling on the past; I am learning from my experiences.

Slowly and steadily, I'm finally beginning to unravel the tangled netting of my life and setting free that which is not a good catch. And gradually, I'll leave it behind. But for now, I'll learn.

Time

One of the things I love about sobriety and self-compassion is time. I've found that as the days have gone by, time has become oh so precious to me. Although I can never get back the days, months, and years I lost through alcoholism, drug addiction, anger, guilt, depression, envy, etc., I can, however, use the time I have left to cultivate joy, understanding, compassion, love, support, knowledge, and a drive to do better. To be better!

It is never too late to embody these positive actions and emotions and teach our young people that there can be a different way. The cycle can only be broken if we do what is required, and as adults, it is our responsibility to do so. I've made so many mistakes in my past; I've hurt many people and cast many judgements. But guilt is an unproductive emotion. I cannot change the past, so carrying it on my shoulders is a pointless endeavour. But what can I do? What can we all do? We can use those experiences not as a means to bring us down, but instead as a foundation to build a positive pathway for our children to follow into a bright future that offers stability, love, security, and joy.

Time is important and I love it!

Because it reminds me, *Matt, if you're going to do something to change, then you'd better do it now, because the clock is ticking and you need to break the cycle!*

Tick, tock, tick, tock, tick, tock ...

Your Failures Are Not the End of Your Story

When we begin to achieve, we can attain success ... but success was not built on achievement alone. In order for us to achieve, we must have failed at some point. In fact, every success was built on failure. So when we fail, what is the most productive solution? Should we give up? Quit? Walk away? Or can we see failure as an opportunity to learn, to strengthen ourselves, and to grow?

You have two options: option 1 – accept defeat and stay as you are, allowing your mistakes to control your future.

Or option 2 – don't quit and strive for better, allowing your mistakes to help you build a brighter future. It's all about perspective and mindset. Our mistakes can form the foundation for our success – for your success! – if you're willing to learn from them and put into action what you have learnt. It's not time to sit on your bum! Change will not happen unless you work for it.

Mindset

Mindset is one of the most powerful tools I have in my recovery tool bag. When I began this journey – and I'm still only at the beginning; I'm well aware of this – I had a word with myself. In one of my wallowing moments, I repeated phrases in my mind like:

Why do I do this?

Why can't I change?

It's so hard!

Then another voice came, one I hadn't heard for a long time, and it said:

PREPARATION! MOTIVATION! DETERMINATION! CONSISTENCY!

A light bulb came on in my mind. *Matt, what the fuck are you doing? Matt, get a grip!*

I can't sit back and allow my issues to overrun me anymore, to destroy my personality and decide my future. I need to take my life by the horns and face things head on!

So alone I sat down and I got strategic. I read and learnt about my issues. I found the discipline I had instilled many years ago in the army and was able to apply it to my situation now.

What do we do – fight on our own ground or take the battle to them? That's what I did in my mind. I called it attacking my problem. How best to attack it?

MINDSET.

I knew I would need to begin changing the patterns of negative behaviour that had become consistent within my life.

So what did I do?

Small goals and projects, because I knew they would form a solid foundation for me to build on. I put pen to paper. Alone, I wrote the life I want and decided that this was my new focus. I popped it on the fridge where I could see it every day.

KNOW YOUR ENEMY.

I decided first to work on my cravings and triggers. Again, I put pen to paper. Making myself aware of what I was battling daily would give me the upper hand and help me pre-empt attacks.

Regularly applying the mindfulness technique of S.T.O.P. – stop, take a breath, observe, proceed – I became able to stand my ground and gained the upper hand. Then I realised through the studying and reading I was doing that alcohol, drugs, and anger were the symptoms, and I needed to work on the root causes. I came to the conclusion that I had experienced a lot of trauma in my life that I had never healed from.

From attempted murder to child sex abuse, the loss of my own child, abandonment, the list goes on. The new weapon in my armoury became talking and sharing. Having the courage to be open about these experiences has given me a new strength and greater confidence in my future pathway and, as a by-product ... my kid's future pathway!

Finding My Voice

Learning to talk about the experiences of my past has been like a weight lifting from my heart. When I was younger, I feared opening up and looking for support or counselling for what I went through. The nights were especially hard for me, and I chose to self-medicate with alcohol and drugs simply to get me through. Over time, this became a normal behaviour pattern for me until it was so ingrained, I could not get through the night without alcohol.

I would get anxious and fear the evenings. But I never really understood why, although I am learning now. I wish I'd had the strength to seek help when I was younger, as I lost a lot of years to my addictions, chained to my past experiences that were not my fault.

I want YOU to know YOU are not alone!

There is help and support out there from caring organisations and people who will not judge but will try to understand how *you* feel. It's never too late to begin living the life you were born to and not the one inflicted on you by someone else.

I just want you to know this ...

I am proud of the person you are, and I know that one day your light will touch the Earth and you will find your way. We are not victims; we are here, we are survivors, and we will stand together showing the world what true strength, integrity, and compassion is.

Our Past Does Not Have to Define Our Future

Forty years passed before I found my voice, which I believe has finally given me the strength, determination, and motivation to climb out of the whirlpool of addiction. As a baby, I experienced my mother walking out, leaving my brother and I, never to be seen again by us. As a child, I witnessed violence that no child should see.

As a child and a teenager, I was raped and sexually as well as psychologically abused repeatedly over a six-year period. I was also attacked and left for dead for no reason whatsoever. In my mind, I had no worth, and in my heart, a darkness gathered that would not allow the warmth of the world to comfort its tears. I found my comfort in alcohol, drugs, and solvents.

Because via these easily available weapons of mass destruction I would find escape.

At least that is how it felt. However, what I really received was further torment, giving my traumas a power over me that they did not deserve. It took me forty years to find my voice, and now I want to tell you this. There are people who will listen, support, and care. The world is not as cold as it feels. You are not alone; together we will be heard. Take my hand and walk with me, proud as the survivor you are!

Hello, my friend. My name is Matthew Penn and I am a recovering alcoholic, addict, and survivor of abandonment, child sexual abuse, and attempted murder. I speak not only for myself but for you and for all survivors when I say listen, believe, understand, and never judge. My traumas were my gateway to addictions that led to behaviours society could not understand. I know my mistakes and wrongdoings, and I am making amends and at peace within myself.

All I ask is that you try to understand the pathway that led me there and see those who suffer with addiction as people and not as society has labelled us for so long. We all have a past, and we are more than those pathways.

They do not have to define our future.

Never Give Up!

Our greatest weakness lies in giving up. The most certain way to succeed is to try just one more time. Treat every obstacle as a new challenge and each mistake as a learning experience. Don't see it as a setback or failure. Every time you get back up again, it is another part of your personal journey that will, in time, make you stronger. Never give up! Keep on going!

Today is a new day, and with every new day comes a new opportunity for the change you desire. Everyone's recovery is different; it's a personal journey and challenge that ultimately comes down to the choices you make. No one can walk that path for you. And yes, it can be the hardest path you ever walk.

I tell you, my friend, that anything worthwhile is never an easy road. But the hardest part of this particular journey is taking the first step. It's the most important step of your life, and it will serve to be the most valuable if you can only commit!

Printed in Great Britain
by Amazon

64569805R00097